THE
Encyclopedia
OF
Dim-Mak

Erle Montaigue
and Wally Simpson

THE
Encyclopedia
OF
Dim-Mak

The Extra Meridians,
Points, and More

PALADIN PRESS • BOULDER, COLORADO

Also by Erle Montaigue:

Advanced Dim-Mak: The Finer Points of Death-Point Striking

Dim-Mak: Death-Point Striking

Dim-Mak's 12 Most Deadly Katas: Points of No Return

The Encyclopedia of Dim-Mak: The Main Meridians

Secrets of Dim-Mak: An Instructional Video

Power Taiji

Ultimate Dim-Mak: How to Fight a Grappler and Win

The Encyclopedia of Dim-Mak:
The Extra Meridians, Points, and More
by Erle Montaigue and Wally Simpson

Copyright © 1997 by Erle Montaigue and Wally Simpson

ISBN 0-87364-928-1
Printed in the United States of America

Published by Paladin Press, a division of
Paladin Enterprises, Inc., P.O. Box 1307,
Boulder, Colorado 80306, USA.
(303) 443-7250

Direct inquiries and/or orders to the above address.

PALADIN, PALADIN PRESS, and the "horse head" design
are trademarks belonging to Paladin Enterprises and
registered in the United States Patent and Trademark Office.

Visit our Web site at www.paladin-press.com

Contents

Warning

On Misuse of this Information

The techniques discussed in this book can be extremely dangerous and even deadly. It is not the intent of the author or publisher to encourage readers to attempt any of them without proper professional supervision and training. Attempting to do so can result in severe injury or death. Do not attempt any of the techniques described without the supervision of a certified instructor or acupuncturist.

The author and publisher disclaim any liability from any damage or injuries of any type that a reader or user of information contained within this book may encounter from the use of said information. *This book is for information purposes only.*

On Plagiarism

The information on dim-mak provided in this book is protected under international copyright law and may not be used in any other publication without permission from the author. This statement is necessary here to because there are those who will consider plagiarizing the information—changing it slightly, perhaps—and then claiming that it was common knowledge. However, the information on dim-mak in this book is not common knowledge, as this is the first time it has ever been presented in physical form. Prior to this publication, this knowledge was only ever passed on by word of mouth and personal teaching from master to student. So when any of the dim-mak point information turns up in other publications, it shall be clear where it came from, no matter how hard the plagiarizer tries to hide the fact.

Anyone who wishes to include this information in any other format or publication, be it a national magazine, an in-house newsletter, a book, or any other media, must contact the author, Erle Montaigue, prior to doing so. In most cases permission will be granted just as long as acknowledgment of the information's origin is included.

INTRODUCTION

In this volume, I present mainly the extraordinary or extra meridians (*mai*). These include the *ren*, the *du*, the *chong*, the *dai*, the *yin wei*, the *yang wei*, the *yin qiao*, and the *yang qiao*. These extra meridians have their own separate pathways, and their points "roam" over the main meridians, holding everything together like rubber bands encircling the body. The points along these meridians are probably my favorite area of dim-mak; they offer a broader scope for experimentation because they are less rigidly placed. They are called extraordinary meridians because they differ from the main meridians in the following ways.

- **The eight extra meridians are not represented by any *zhang fu* (internal bodily organs, such as the heart).**
  The 12 main meridians are each represented by an internal organ.

- **The eight extra meridians are not externally/internally related.**
  The 12 extra meridians are externally/internally related.

- **The eight extra meridians have no points of their own; they use those on other meridians that they cross.**
  The 12 main meridians all have their own points and names for those points.

- **The distribution of the eight extra meridians runs from the lower parts of the body to the upper (except for the chong and dai mai).**
  The distribution of the 12 main meridians runs both upward and downward.

- **The eight extra meridians have no distribution with the upper limbs.**
  The 12 main meridians have distribution to both the upper and lower limbs.

- **Of the eight extra meridians, half are single meridians (the du, ren, chang, and dai), while the other half (the yin qiao, yin wei, yang qiao, and yang wei) are distributed in pairs.**
  All of the 12 main meridians are in pairs, on either side of the body.

The eight extra meridians' courses are distributed along the 12 main meridians. They function in regulating the blood and qi circulation of the main meridians. Should there be an excess of qi and blood in the main meridians, it is infused into the extra meridians and stored there until needed by the main meridians.

The extra meridians divide the body into eight areas. The ren mai, or conceptor vessel (Cv), and the du mai, or governing vessel (Gv), divide the left and right sides of the body. The dai mai divides the upper and lower parts of the body. The gallbladder and triple heater meridians (which share many points with the extra meridians) are used to divide the front and back of the yang aspect of the body, and the liver and pericardium meridians (which also share many points with the extra meridians) divide the front and back of the yin aspect.

The first two meridians covered are the conceptor vessel and the governing vessel. They differ from the six other extra meridians in that they have their own points and names for those points, whereas the other six meridians are considered to be linking meridians whose points take their names from those on other meridians they cross. Even though the Cv and Gv are considered two of the eight extra meridians, acupuncture books always lump them in with the main meridians because they are so important. This is true not only in acupuncture but also in dim-mak. In fact, there are more deadly points on these two meridians than on any other single meridian.

The points on the conceptor vessel and the governing vessel are dangerous because they form the centerline of the body. The center of the body means a great deal more in Chinese medicine than it does in Western medicine. It also means a whole lot more in dim-mak because we are able to disrupt the entire balance of the body by striking to points along the centerline of the upper body. Most great martial arts, including Bruce Lee's system, placed a great deal of significance upon the centerline—in other words, along the Cv and the Gv meridians.

When points along these meridians are struck, it causes a split in the energies of the body, like opening up a great chasm down the center of the body, energy-wise. Once this occurs, depending upon what we do next, we can further disrupt the energy by causing the different parts of the body to change polarity, i.e., the left side of the body can be made more yang than the right side, thus upsetting the whole body so much that it could cause death.

If we then strike, for instance, at the upper part of the centerline meridians, we can completely upset the energy flow to that part, thus creating confusion in the brain. The opposite happens when we strike to the lower parts of the centerline meridians: we cause confusion in the legs. Should we strike to the center of the centerline meridians, Cv 14 or Gv 11, death almost certainly happens because we have completely disrupted the whole body's energy flow. We have not only attacked the centerline meridians, we have attacked right in the center of those meridians. This would be like dropping a bomb on New York City rather than on a small outlying town.

The six other meridians are generally the source of most of our multiple point strikes (when we strike two or more points in a single application). Because these six meridians use points from the 12 main meridians, you will see that although you are using points on, for instance, the yang qiao mai, you are actually using points on several of the main meridians, which makes for very dangerous multiple point strikes. There are, of course, combinations that aren't on the extra meridians, but taking points from the extra meridians and using them in combination is an easy way to remember where the most deadly multiple point strikes are, because the extra meridians run over the most deadly combinations of main meridian points, all of which are linked by the extra meridians.

In covering the ren mai and the du mai, I will use the same format I used for the 12 main meridians. But when I get to the other extra meridians, I will simply be covering multiple point strikes on each, along with their effects, antidotes, and so on. I will give only the names of the points in the attack and where it begins and ends, since the locations were covered in the first volume. (You will also know where these points are located by the names.) I will also touch on the healing aspects of each, although I will focus mainly on their dim-mak context; there are some excellent books already out there on the eight extra meridians for healing. There are probably more healing applications using multiple points on the extra meridians than the main meridians. In fact, many Chinese doctors specialize in the use of the eight extra meridians only (keeping in mind, of course, that the points of the six linking meridians are "regular" points anyway). For those interested in the healing side of the art in general, an introduction to traditional Chinese medicine (TCM) follows, written by Wally Simpson, one of my students and a highly accomplished acupuncturist.

The extra meridians are particularly susceptible to magnetic changes. Changes in geomagnetic areas will cause changes in the body, and strikes that create a magnetic force in the body, such as in "qi disruptive" methods, will also affect the extra meridians and, thus, the balance of the whole body. In treating the extra meridians, we are mainly treating balance disorders. It is said that treating the extra meridians will cure many physical disorders involving imbalance, such as tension and even uneven (one longer or shorter) legs and arms, for instance. And in striking to multiple points on these meridians, we are causing extreme imbalances internally and also physically.

In addition to the extra meridians, I will also cover the extra and new points. These are points that are either not situated on any particular meridian (extra) or those that have been discovered in relatively modern times (new). Not all of these points are suitable for dim-mak, so I have included only those that I know work well and those that are relatively easy to get at.

The chapter entitled "The Medical Aspects of the Martial Arts" presents what medical science has to say about striking to certain points and gives evidence about why some of the points in dim-mak work. In fact, many of the modern day *tuite* (Japanese word for dim-mak) teachers have gained much knowledge from this area. Evidence to show why the St 9 shot works so well, or why the shot to Cv 17 works so well, as in the "heart knockout," is given by doctors from as far back as the 1800s.

It's all very well reading this book and learning where the points are, how to use them, and why they work, but it's also nice to have someone give you some idea about what points work the best, especially since the readers of this book range from novices right up to highly ranked karateka. So I've included a chapter on my favorite points and combinations of points—their effects, how to use them, and so on.

The "Internal Methods" chapter takes everything you have learned from this book and raises it a level into the "internal," covering things like being able to direct your qi to certain parts of the body, for instance, even though you might have punched several inches away from the main target. As examples, you can attack the brain by striking to the upper chest, and you can attack the heart even though you have struck to the chin or the lower abdomen.

As the results of training increase, certain things happen to the body and mind—things we wish to teach others, but that are perhaps a bit too esoteric or so internal that there is no way of expressing them physically so that people can learn. To address this dilemma, I have opened the Erle Montaigue Research Institute for the Internal Arts. Here, I am taking everything I have learned from doing and trying to find ways of giving others this knowledge in a much shorter time than it took me to learn it. As part of this research, I have completed two papers, which I have incorporated into this volume. Those who are more advanced will use this information to bond together various random thoughts that they might have had without any way of linking all the information together. Many of you will perhaps only read them and not gain much. But as the results of your own training increase, you will think back to what you read in this book and immediately know what it is you are feeling and why.

Introduction to Traditional Chinese Medicine

by Wally Simpson

The first thing I discovered about massage was that if I felt good about doing it, then the person on the receiving end felt good about getting it. This was basic Swedish massage. These days I'm not sure all my clients feel good about getting massage from me, but the majority of them feel good about the results. You don't have to be a professional to give a good massage, as long you feel good about doing it.

I never felt good about doing martial arts; it always seemed a brutal, aggressive sort of thing to do. I was much more into communication with nature through surfing, bush walking, and so on, and though surfing could get a little aggressive at times, it was just the child in us demanding our birthright. (Every wave that we wanted, on our own.) It wasn't in the same league as martial arts, or so I thought. (Isn't youthful innocence amazing?)

Then, after earning a degree in Traditional Chinese Medicine (TCM), I decided that to be the complete doctor of TCM I had to teach people how to heal themselves and stay healthy via life-style (e.g., exercise, diet). Well, the Chinese did t'ai chi, and I was told that t'ai chi is not a martial art, and it didn't look all that aggressive to me. So off I went to learn this new skill. After three years of studying t'ai chi with what I thought was a reputable organization, I was introduced to one of Erle Montaigue's students, who told me that t'ai chi was a martial art and what I was doing looked nice but it wasn't t'ai chi. The concept of t'ai chi as a martial art wasn't easy for me to digest, but after my first lesson in the Yang Cheng-fu form, I knew it was far ahead of what I had been taught as t'ai chi. I guess it took the next 10 to 12 months for me to feel good about doing the small san-sou as well as the form, and it would be two years before I would meet Erle in person (though I had seen him at a couple of camps). Now, after training with Erle personally for three years, I know that it was one of the best things I have ever been fortunate enough to become involved with, and the martial stuff I was so apprehensive about has changed my life for the better in a way that I never could have imagined. It has given me a lot of confidence in myself and in my ability to defend myself and family, as well as to help others toward health and happiness. It has also improved my capacity to heal.

What Erle has given me with t'ai chi was like a seed that sprouted and is now in the process of growing into what will be a source of nourishment for myself, my family, and my many clients and friends for many, many years.

It is a great honor and a privilege to coauthor this book with Erle. The research has taken a large part of my spare time, but the information that I have unearthed (some of it rediscovered) has made it well worthwhile. I hope you gain as much out of these pages as I have. Thanks, Erle, for the opportunity once again for growth.

THE ENERGY MERIDIANS

The belief that the body is traversed by channels of energy and that this energy is the driving force behind the functions and movements of the various organs, muscles, tissue, and cells of all living creatures has been taught by many ancient cultures and has persisted from the earliest times to the present. Nowadays, modern scientists, especially physicists, are discovering through their scientific investigations that these ancient beliefs hold many more truths than was previously believed.

The Chinese called these channels of energy "meridians." In addition to the 12 main meridians covered in the first volume, there are also eight extra meridians (including the Cv and Gv channels) covered in this volume, *luo* (connecting) channels, tendino muscular channels (relating to the tendons and muscles that relate to the 12 main meridians), and divergent (distinct) channels.

Over many thousands of years the Chinese discovered that these meridians could be influenced, both beneficially and adversely, at certain points along their pathways. Modern science has found that these points, when scanned with apparatuses that measure electrical charge, have a reduced capacity for conductivity. These points are like mini-vortexes of energy spiraling into our body's major energy channels. When struck in a certain way, punctured with needles, pressed, tapped, or rotated, they have a specific effect on both local muscle, tissue, and cells, and other areas enervated, traversed, or influenced by the particular meridian being dealt with by the different methods of intervention.

HEALING AND MASSAGE

Healing and massage are very much like martial arts; you must move from your center to have real power.

When a martial artist throws a punch and uses only the power from the muscles of his or her arm, the punch lacks any real power, and its penetration will be relatively shallow. Likewise, in massage, if you are just using your arms or hands to perform different techniques, the penetration will only reach the surface muscles, and after you have done three or four one-hour massages you will find that your arms and hands are starting to feel heavy and tired. Whereas, if the movements are coming from your waist or, more specifically, *tantien*, you will find that you can massage all day, and when you go home in the evening you will feel quite invigorated. Your techniques will reach farther into the body to the deeper layers of muscles and tendons, as there is more strength and penetration with movements from the waist.

Your stance is important. I was using a horse stance, but lately I have been using the power stance from advanced push-hands. Whatever your stance, the back should be as straight as possible. Depending on the height of your table and the size of your client, the knees should also be bent. I find that using a slightly lower table is best, so that if clients are quite big and solid, you can get over the top of them without standing on tiptoes, which allows your to bring more weight to bear on the area being worked. With a thin client, the knees can be bent more to keep the back straight. Breathing should be low in the tantien and, if possible, in sync with the person receiving the massage.

You must be able to react to a large variety of variables and respond with the type of movement needed for the present circumstances in both martial art and massage. To have a set approach and be unwilling to modify that approach with different clients/conditions is to severely limit the quality of the results you will achieve. It's like knowing only one or two strikes or blocks from a martial art form: if you are good at them, then you will succeed at times; if you know the whole form and are good at it, you will succeed a lot more. So try lots of different approaches to the same types of conditions in your massage and be flexible in how to treat. Listen to your clients—not just their voices, but what the muscles and points/channels are telling you. Work from both sides of the table, just as you should do martial techniques on both sides to keep your body in balance and be capable of using both hands/legs/feet. If you work only from one side of the table with massage, you will become unbalanced (the lumbar vertebra rotate in the direction you constantly lean) and need treatment yourself.

If you work on the floor, the same principles apply. Work from both sides and bring the movements from your tantien. To do this it is best to kneel beside the client. If you are sitting you can't move well, from your tantien. To do this it is best to kneel beside the client. If you are sitting you can't move well, and you both suffer as a result.

You need to clear your mind of the chatter that normally goes on in there, and focus your attention on what you *intend* to achieve. That is not to say that you massage while spacing out, thinking, "I am going to heal this person" or "I am building yin or yang." Rather, it implies that you have a clear mind and an intention to build yin or yang and heal the individual. It's as in the martial arts—if there is no intent behind a movement, then results are poor. Without intent, there is very little chance of either a strike or a massage technique being successful. In the martial arts, we hear and read a lot about this "no mind" state, where the reptilian brain takes over and there is no conscious control over actions. Well, before that state is reached there must first be intent. A crocodile uses intent as a focus to provide the power and direction for that lunge up the river bank to grab its prey and drag it back to the water—just as you must intend to learn a martial art, or no amount of lessons can turn you into a martial artist. You must intend to help your clients, or no amount of massage will bring them relief from their symptoms.

When you are working with people in a healing capacity, it is possible to pick up negative energy from them, especially if you feel the healing is coming *from* you rather than through you. The *no mind* state mentioned above is the best way to stop that absorption of negative energy. In that state, you become a channel, and that allows energy to flow *through* you, not from you. The no mind state is what allows us to be free of attachment to the outcome. In healing, this means the client can proceed at his or her own pace with healing. It's a bit like saying, "Okay, here is a way out of this mess; I'll open the door, and you walk through when you are ready." Without attachment to the outcome, there is no draining of your energy and, as a result, little likelihood of your picking up negative energy. As martial artists, too, this lack of attachment to the outcome allows us to be ready for whatever happens, and that is a very important contribution to the final outcome.

The point Gv 20 (*baihui*), on top of the head (*sahasrara chakra* in the yogic tradition), is an entry and exit point for qi, as is Kd 1. It is said that the yang qi of heaven condenses and falls to earth to become yin qi, while the yin qi of earth evaporates to rise and become the yang qi of heaven. Mankind stands between heaven and earth and is subject to the qi of both. Yang qi of heaven enters via Gv 20 and exits via Kd 1; yin qi of earth enters via Kd 1 and exits via Gv 20. *Laogong* (Pc 8) is another point where qi can enter and exit the body. Likewise, Gv 4 (*mingmen*) is seen as the point of entry for yang qi at birth.

There are many other points for entry and exit of qi from the body, but those are the only ones I'll mention here. It is a good idea to free up those points so that when you are doing massage or healing work, the qi will flow through you without any effort on your part. The qi of heaven and earth meet in the middle at the *dai mai* (girdle or belt meridian) and can be directed out of Pc 8 to help another being or harm another being, depending on your *intent*. Doing qigong will eventually make you aware of these points, and that is the first step in freeing them up. We have these pathways open anyway, but most of us tend to isolate ourselves from them with the business of the everyday world.

So we have all this healing and martial stuff happening in the no mind state, and it is our intent that gives us direction and impetus. But intent without the ability is like sex without the partner; it mainly happens in your mind. So make sure you do the training to back what you intend to achieve. With massage, this means not only reading and learning how to locate points and what they do, but also doing lots of massage so your hands develop a feel for different conditions.

METHODS OF LOCATING POINTS

There are three methods of measuring where the points are located.

Anatomical Landmarks
The first way is to use physical landmarks such as a depression or a prominence of the bones, a joint or a muscle, the edge of the nail, a skin crease, the hairline, the area between the nipples or to the nipple, the umbilicus, the corner of the mouth or eyes, or a tendon.

Proportional Measurement

A second method is to take the different parts of the body and divide them proportionally. Each division is termed *one cun* (pronounced *tsoone*). For example, the distance from the second finger joint to the first is one cun (diagram 1). The one cun measurement will differ from a large person to a smaller person, as it is taken from anatomical parts of each individual's body.

On the head we have several measurements: from the anterior hairline to the posterior hairline is 12 cun (diagram 2); between the two mastoid processes is 9 cun, as is the distance between both St 8 points.

On the chest we usually base the measurements upon the intercostal spaces, or those between the ribs. From the axillary fold to the 11th rib is 12 cun. From the sternocostal angle to the middle of the navel is 8 cun. From the navel to the upper line of the symphysis pubis is 5 cun. Between the two nipples is 8 cun (diagram 3). Between the scapular medial line and the posterior midline is 3 cun.

On the arm, from the end of the axillary fold to the transverse cubital crease is 9 cun (diagram 4). On the forearm, the distance between the transverse cubital crease (elbow) and the carpal crease (wrist) is 12 cun (diagram 5).

On the thigh (diagram 6), the distance from the pubis to the medial epicondyle of the femur is 18 cun. From the prominence of the greater trochanter on the outside of the thigh to the center of the patella is 19 cun.

For more minute measurements, we use *fen*, which denotes one-tenth of a cun.

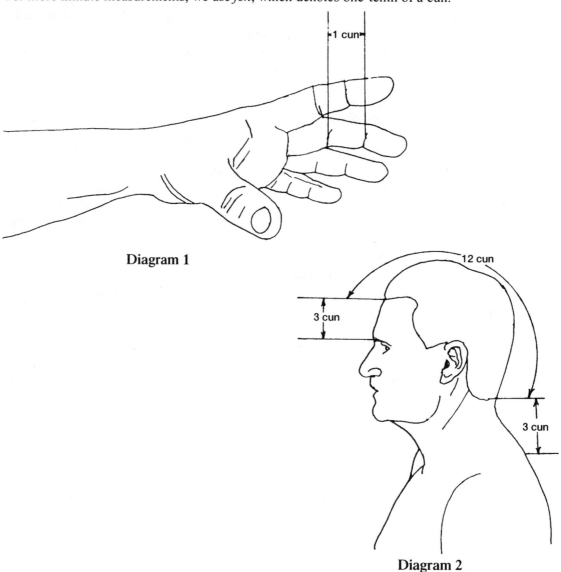

Diagram 1

Diagram 2

8

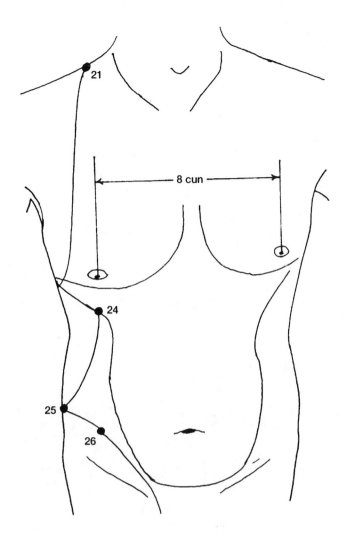

Diagram 3

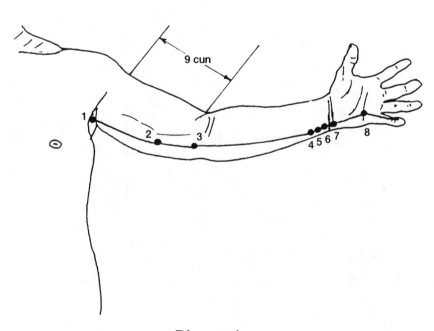

Diagram 4

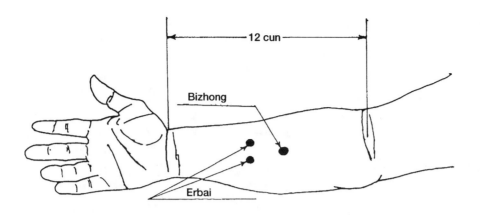

Diagram 5

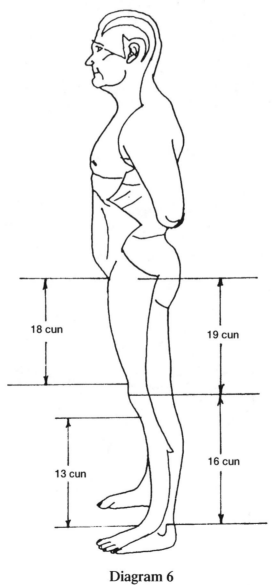

Diagram 6

Measuring with the Fingers

Finally, we use the fingers to locate the points.

When the longest finger is flexed, the distance between the two ends of the creases of the interphalangeal joints is one cun.

The width of the four fingers when they are held together is 3 cun (diagram 7). The width of the thumb is one cun. The width of the index and longest finger taken at the second joint is 1.5 cun.

You might notice a seeming inconsistency between some of the measurements and what you see in the diagrams. For instance, the measurement across the forehead, when looked at on a two-dimensional diagram (diagram 8), looks as if it is not actually 9 cun—in fact, it looks like much less. However, you have to take into consideration that this measurement goes around the forehead from St 8 to St 8. So when you take a piece of string and stretch it from St 8 to St 8, then place that length from nipple to nipple, the distance between which is 8 cun, then you will see that the forehead distance is indeed 9 cun.

Because the Chinese way of measuring depends upon the size of the patient, it is best if you have the experience to know automatically where the points are and only use the measurements as a rough guide. Most acupuncturists prefer to use the anatomical method.

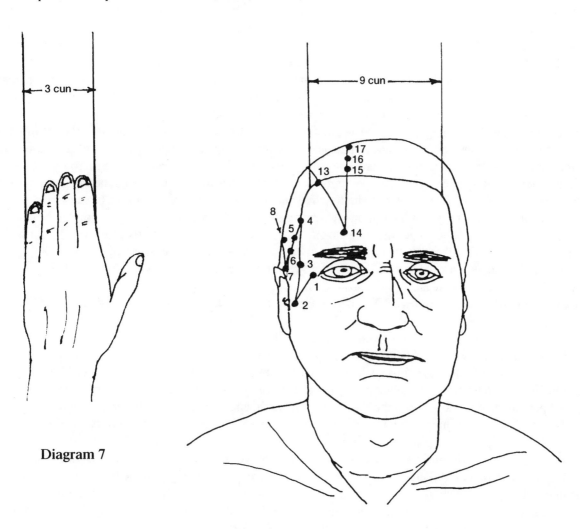

Diagram 7

Diagram 8

STATES OF UNWELLNESS: THE UNDERLYING CAUSES

The Chinese believe that it is some type of disruption to the flow of energy that creates all states of unwellness. Thus, when looking at the cause of a disease, a TCM doctor looks at several broad classifications of conditions. These broad classifications are then further refined by consideration of the syndromes of the organs (*zhang/fu*) or channels and collaterals (*jing/lou*) involved. In the text that follows, we will take a look at those that have the most significance for our purposes in this text.

Xu (Deficient) and Shi (Excess) Conditions

Xu, or deficient conditions, are characterized by weakness, decrease in body function, listless spirit, lethargy, shortness of breath, aversion to speaking, and poor appetite. Pain are dull, vague aches that improve with massage, and you may feel coldness in the problem areas. The face and complexion may be pale, as is the body of the tongue. The tongue may also appear swollen and have scalloped sides. The pulse feels weak.

The "emptiness" (*xu*) may be of qi, *xue* (blood), yin, or yang. Yin xu causes a rapid and weak pulse, and the tongue body may appear red with no coating or a patchy coating. Patients may have a subjective feeling of heat, especially in the afternoon and evenings, or they may have hot flashes and night sweating and appear wasted. Yang xu produces a slow, weak pulse and the tongue body will be moist and may have a thick coating on its surface. Patients may feel cold or cool, even on hot days.

Xu conditions are nourished or tonified with massage that involves clockwise rotations; strong, deep, even pressure; and slow movements in the direction of the channel flow, that is, from the small numbers to the large numbers (referring to the numbers assigned to the acupuncture points along the meridian.)

Xu conditions feel empty on the surface, and as you get deeper you will find an area of consolidation. They often present themselves as flaccid muscles or a depression over the point/area, or even as a wasting of the whole muscle tissue in that region. They are generally pale and feel cooler than surrounding tissue, and the client is likely to report a lack of energy or lethargy either in the area or in general. These areas, while they may be sore and ache, like to be touched and like heat; they are less likely to cause restriction of movement than other types of conditions. Clients will probably experience them as a dull ache or a weakness. Work more slowly over these areas; start gently and move deeper fairly rapidly. While it will probably hurt, clients will report that it is a nice pain; they like to be touched, pushed, and prodded in these areas, so you can stay deeper for longer. As a result, you can generally work there until significant improvement is achieved. Heat, and in particular moxibustion, is wonderful in these types of conditions. Moxibustion is the burning of herbs. The herb mugwart is cured for a long period, made into a stick, and burned on or near acupoints or on needles. Moxa warms cold and builds qi and yang via penetration of heat energy. Moxa is very good to use on yang xu patients.

In xu conditions, where cold and lethargy are a problem, in addition to treating local points/areas with moxa, it is a good idea to use points such as Kd 3, Sp 3, St 36, Bl 23, Bl 20, Th 4, Gv 4, Cv 4, Gv 6, Gv 12, and Gb 25 to help build qi and yang in general. It is yang qi that acts as the first line of defense against pathogenic invasion, cooks the food in the stomach, and extracts the nutrient and sends it up to join with the qi from the air we breathe. Yang qi provides us with warmth and the ability to process fluids, as well as holding things in place and supplying the get up and go for our everyday activity.

Excess, or *shi* conditions may be the result of a strong external pathogen (e.g., wind, cold, heat, dryness, damp, fire, trauma) attacking a weakened system and penetrating into the body, causing it to become full of perverse energy. These conditions may also occur due to normal body conditions and a very excessive set of circumstances, or as a result of holding onto an emotion for a long time and thus stagnating the free flow of energy (of which emotions are a part).

Shi conditions tend to be of recent onset, acute, and of short duration. Patients may be in good spirits, have a flushed face and a loud voice, and have very severe pain that feels worse with pressure and doesn't particularly like massage. Muscles may appear to be in spasm and rigid and may rebound when pressed. Other signs and symptoms will depend upon what type of fullness is presenting. For instance, heat will cause a redness of both the area involved and the tongue body. The coating on the tongue may be thick and yellow, or black if the condition is very severe. The pulse will be rapid and strong, as is standard in shi conditions. The damaged area or the whole body may feel hot to touch, and there may be a great thirst.

Shi conditions are sedated or dispersed with massage that involves counterclockwise rotations and fast, lighter movements against the flow of the channel (i.e., from the largest numbers to the small numbers.) From my experience, I have found that some individuals with shi conditions of the muscles—where the muscle is hard as a rock and feels bloody awful when pressed—get best results from massage if they concentrate on their breathing and let the doctor work quite deeply. Concentrating on the breathing helps to deal with the pain being inflicted by the massage technique and also helps release the blockage of energy or blood (qi or xue) in the muscle.

Excess conditions feel solid or dense all the way up to the surface. The area may look raised, feel hot, and look red or darkish compared to the surrounding tissues. Normally, these are very painful conditions, causing varying amounts of restriction to movement. They do not like to be touched and may not respond to heat (this varies, depending on the type of shi condition and the duration of the condition; it is possible to get a full cold condition, which will respond well to heat). Work quickly and gently at first over these shi regions, but slowly make your movements deeper. Your client will let you know how deep you can go and for how long you can stay there. It is no good getting too deep too soon, because the client will tense excessively and grit the teeth to stop you from penetrating. This may at times be useful, as when clients become super tense and rigid from your pressure; when you stop pressing, they get a greater degree of relaxation. It can also just tense them up and not produce any relaxation at all. Your client has the final say about the depth you can reach. I find it best to work quickly over these areas and come back to them often. Use points that are on the same meridian pathway but that are located on the extremities to help drain stuck qi and blood out of tense areas (e.g., for extremely tight shoulders, treat local points and then use points like Si 3, Gb 34, Gb 41, Gb 43, Gb 44, Co 4, Bl 60, etc., as distal points).

In shi conditions where there has been a penetration of cold that has resulted in muscle spasm and pain (e.g., wind/cold penetration into the muscles and channels of the neck and shoulders), use points like Gv 14 to warm the cold and free up the channels or Gb 21 to warm the cold and send stagnant qi back down to be dispersed. For cold to have penetrated, there has either been an underlying xu condition or an exposure to extremes of cold over an extended period. So you may need to tonify xu with the above-mentioned points, as well as disperse the cold, warm the yang, and free up the channels.

Some points can sedate shi (excess) as well as tonify xu (deficient) conditions. So you need to be clear on what you are working with.

Internal and External Climatic Conditions
Other factors that influence our lives are the internal and external climatic conditions, and if we are to be successful at treating disease, then we need to be familiar with these conditions and how they interact within the body's landscape. There are six evils (*liu xie*) or pernicious influences: wind, cold, heat or fire, dryness, dampness, and summer heat. An individual with one or more of these conditions will most probably have an aversion to the particular influence involved.

Wind (*feng*) can be of internal or external origin. Wind seldom attacks the body alone; it is usually in the company of another pathogen, such as heat, cold, or dampness. Wind tends to cause symptoms to appear and disappear suddenly. It produces change and a degree of urgency in what is otherwise slow and even. Wind is a yang phenomenon associated with spring, though it can appear in any season (e.g., hay fever is a classic wind-related disease that most often appears in spring but can appear in autumn). Wind tends to affect the upper parts of the body first—skin, face, neck, sweat glands, lungs, and *taiyang* (the most exterior of the six yin and yang divisions, it includes bladder and small intestine and tends to be seen as the first stage of penetration by external pathogenic influences). Wind can cause spasms, tremors of the limbs, twitching, dizziness, tetany, symptoms such as rash or arthritis, or maybe just pain that moves from one place to another (e.g., shingles). With external wind invasion, some people may recall having been exposed to draught, while others won't. External wind invasion is characterized by its sudden onset. It is often accompanied by fever, as the protective (*wei*) qi fights to expel the invading pathogen. This is more simultaneous chills and fever, with the symptom that predominates signaling the type of pathogen that the wind has combined with.

Internal wind is generally of a chronic nature and often involves the liver (e.g., an excess condition of the liver, such as liver fire, can create wind in the same way as a fire creates an updraft, causing symptoms such as migraine or tinnitus, while a deficient condition of, say, liver blood may create empty wind symptoms, such as itchy eyes). Internal wind may include such symptoms as dizziness, tinnitus, numbness of the limbs, tremors, convulsions, or apoplexy.

Cold (*han*) can be of internal or external origin and of an excess or deficient nature. It is a yin pathogen associated with winter in the same way as wind is associated with spring. It can appear in any season (e.g., a cool breeze in summer can generate an attack of wind cold in the body, especially if there is a preexisting condition or a weakness of defensive qi), though it will be aggravated in cold weather. The most reliable sign is that the individual feels cold—the whole or part of the body will feel cold to the touch and/or it may have a pale, frigid look, and the person will have an aversion to cold and actively seek warmth and warm clothes. Cold causes things to contract and so restricts movement and blocks the circulation of qi in the channels, causing sharp, severe cramping pain that will generally respond positively to heat. Cold from external attack will cause symptoms such as aversion to cold and acute severe cramping pain that does not like to be touched but likes heat. There may be chills and fever, with the chills predominating. The pulse will be slow and feel full and floating (it can be felt better at the superficial levels with light touch), the tongue will be pale and moist with a thin white coating (this coating may be thick if there is a lot of damp or phlegm present). There will be body aches, headache, and usually only small amounts of sweating if there is any at all (cold obstructs the pores).

Internal cold is the result of a deficient yang qi. Yang qi is hot and active, so a decline in it causes the body to become cold and slow. Internal cold is generally associated with chronic conditions or the consumption of too much raw or cold food and drink. It is generally related to the kidney or the spleen. Symptoms might include slow, weak pulse; aversion to cold; and a preference for hot drinks and warm clothes. Patients generally like to be touched and respond well to heat. The tongue is pale and moist and has a thin white or patchy coating (or it may have a thick white coating because there is no heat for digestion). Movements will be slow and weak, and there may be copious clear urine and loose stool with food in it (maybe watery stool), discharges will be white or clear and have little or no smell, and the patient may sleep curled up in a fetal position and have a lack of energy, poor digestion, and a slow, deep pulse.

Hot (*re*) or fire (*huo*) can be internal or external in origin and can be of an excess or deficient nature. It is a yang pathogen and, though associated with summer, can occur in any season. Heat is normal in the body; it is the yang aspect that creates activity and warmth for the body. As a pathogenic influence, it causes either the whole body or part of the body to feel hot and to have a red color. The hot pathogen may create irritability and agitation, the patient will dislike heat and prefer cold drinks, and there may be signs of high fever, chills and fever where heat predominates, as well as a red face and a red tongue with a yellow dry or yellow greasy coating, depending on what it combines with (e.g., dryness or damp). The pulse will be rapid; if it is an external pathogen the pulse will also be floating. There will generally be a big thirst, maybe lots of sweating, and perhaps foul-smelling urine/secretions. Urine will be yellow (check that it is not just from vitamin B intake), and the stool may be dry and constipated or loose and smelly (can be explosive). If the pathogen is excess, then it won't like touch, whereas if deficient it will like touch. There may be extravasation of blood (e.g., bloody nose, hematuria).

Heat causes things to dry out, so there can be a lack of or scanty excretions. External excess heat invasion can produce a fast/full/floating pulse, forceful/severe pains, convulsions, very hot dry symptoms, excess thirst, lots of sweat or no sweat, great irritability, and possibly delirium.

Internal heat/fire can be excess or deficient in nature. If excess, it is usually contracted from the liver. The major symptoms of the pathology of liver fire flaring include sudden outbursts of anger, red eyes, irritability, inability to keep still, and violent migraines. Most if not all excess internal heat/fire is the result of emotional suppression or stagnation. Internal excess of liver heat may also result in heavy or irregular periods.

Internal deficient heat or fire is the result of a yin deficiency. There is not enough yin (coolness) to keep the yang (heat, fire) of the body in check, so an apparent excess of yang develops. Deficient heat symptoms include thirst but no desire to drink; red tongue with a thin yellow coating or no coating; afternoon fevers; malar flush; weak, empty, fast pulse; pain that gets better with touch; night sweats; and fear of cold. The flushing of menopause is a deficient heat condition in most cases.

Damp (*shi*) is wet, heavy, and slow. It is a yin pathogen associated with damp, cloudy weather in any season. Living and working in damp surroundings and wearing damp clothes can contribute to a damp condition. A major factor in the generation of damp conditions is the over-consumption of cold food and drink, raw food, or greasy food. Irregular eating habits will weaken the spleen's ability to transform and transport food and fluids effectively. Dampness is heavy, turbid, lingering, and can tend to move things downward, affecting the lower parts of the body first, though when combined with wind, it will affect the upper parts of the body (e.g., headache where the head feels heavy, dull, as though there is a tight band around it). Symptoms could include heavy, sore limbs; excretions and secretions that are often copious, turbid, cloudy, and sticky; eyes that feel as if they have sand in them; urine that is cloudy; stool that could be quite loose or even diarrhea; and maybe heavy vaginal discharge, fluid-filled lesions, or oozing skin eruptions.

External damp may obstruct qi, resulting in fullness in the chest or abdomen and dribbling or incomplete urination and/or defecation. It can also obstruct the qi in the channels causing heaviness, stiffness, and/or soreness and swelling in the joints. If it affects the spleen, it may interfere with the rising of pure qi (extract from food and fluids) and cause loss of appetite, indigestion, nausea, diarrhea, edema, etc. One of the best signs of damp that I come across all the time is when you feel really awful when you first get up after sleep or even just sitting or lying for a while, but start to feel better after moving around a bit. External and internal damp are distinguishable mainly by the speed of onset. External damp is acute and will be accompanied by other external signs; it can easily become internal damp. Internal damp is likely to make the individual more susceptible to external damp. Regardless of where it came from, damp is an insidious pathogen and can last a long time. Mucus or phlegm (*tan*) is a form of internal damp and is generally generated by disharmonies of the spleen and kidney. Dampness can condense when there is heat present or when it has been around for a while. Since phlegm is heavier than damp and much more viscous, it can easily obstruct the channels, generating lumps, nodules, tumors, etc. In the lungs it causes cough with thick expectoration. In the heart it can obstruct the *shen* (spirit), resulting in muddled thought, stupor, coma-type conditions, madness, or chaotic behavior. Mucus in the channels can cause numbness; paralysis; nodules; soft, mobile tumors; and limbs that ache and feel heavy. The tongue most often has a thick, greasy coating when phlegm is present, though it may just be moist in damp conditions. The pulse is slippery in both.

Summer heat (*shu*) is an external pathogen that is the result of exposure to extreme heat. Symptoms include sudden high fever and heavy sweating; if it enters the stomach it causes nausea and vomiting. Summer heat can easily damage the qi, resulting in exhaustion. It can also damage the fluids, causing dryness. Summer heat often occurs with dampness.

Dryness (*zao*) is associated with autumn. It is a yang phenomenon closely related to heat—heat and dryness are on a continuum, dryness toward dehydration and heat toward redness and hotness. Symptoms of dryness include dry mouth, lips, tongue, and nostrils; cracked skin; and dry, hard stool. External dryness can interfere with the descending and dispersing function of the lungs, causing symptoms such as dry cough, little or no sputum, asthma, chest pain, fever, body aches, and other external symptoms.

It is fairly unusual for these types of pathogens, especially when they are of exterior origin, to attack the body on their own. Most often they combine with wind, such as in the case of *bi* syndrome (the Chinese equivalent of arthritis), where wind/cold/damp or wind/heat/damp, etc. get together to retard the flow of qi and xue, causing pain, swelling, and restriction of movement. It is even possible to have an attack of wind/dryness in one area of the body while experiencing a wind/damp heat attack in another part.

THE 5 ELEMENT POINTS CYCLE OF CREATION OR SHENG CYCLE

The sheng/creation or nourishing cycle is where each element nourishes or creates the next cycle (element)—e.g., fire creates earth. The sequence can be rationalized as follows:

Wood creates fire (the wood is burned to create the fire).
Fire creates earth (fire expends itself, and what is left is ash which become earth).
Earth creates metal (the element metal is found by digging in the earth).
Metal creates water (by melting—solid metals melt to form a liquid). Metal also
    corresponds to air (in Western astrology), and air condenses to form a liquid.
Water creates wood (by nourishing growth).

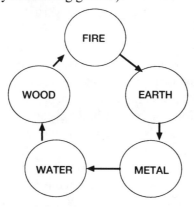

The 5 element points cycle of creation or sheng cycle.

If each element is fed and strengthened, it will feed the next element in the cycle, as a mother feeds a son or daughter; thus it is termed the cycle of creation, and it gives birth to the mother/son theory used in treating disharmonies.

The KO/inhibiting/repressive or controlling cycle is where each element inhibits or controls the element two steps ahead in the sequence. For example, wood controls earth. This is like a grandparent exerting control over a grandchild, and in TCM it is called grandmother/grandson cycle. It works as follows:

Fire controls metal (by melting it).
Metal controls wood (by cutting it).
Wood controls earth (by covering it).
Earth controls water (by damming it).
Water controls fire (by extinguishing it).

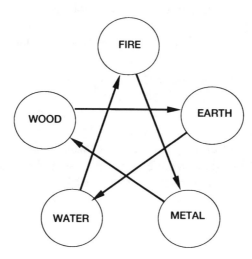

The Ko cycle.

The organ-element relationship is as follows:

ELEMENT	YANG ORGAN	YIN ORGAN
EARTH	STOMACH	SPLEEN
METAL	COLON	LUNGS
WATER	BLADDER	KIDNEYS
WOOD	GALL BLADDER	LIVER
FIRE	SMALL INTESTINE/	HEART/
	TRIPLE HEATER	PERICARDIUM

The harmonious balance of the sheng and KO cycles represents the mutual support and control of the five elements. The sheng (creative) cycle ensures that there is continual growth and generation. The KO cycle ensures that there is growth within limits, that growth does not continue unchecked. Thus the two cycles represent the balance of the five elements. Both cycles are natural and positive, unless an imbalance or blockage occurs in the flow, resulting in the generation of a destructive cycle.

The sheng cycle is predominant during the day, and the KO cycle is predominant during the night. Each element has its corresponding color, smell, body organ/channel, etc. that can form the basis of diagnosis. If any concordance tends to predominate or is lacking, a practitioner will be able to diagnose which part of the sequence is disturbed and treat the energies accordingly to open the natural flows.

Another way of using this system is as follows. An inflammatory condition occurring in an organ or tissue can be seen as a fire-type symptom (feels hot, causes irritation, etc.), so using the water point to reduce this fire (inflammation) can have a dramatic and immediate effect on the inflammation. If the inflammation is not completely relieved by the water point, then add a metal point to nourish the water and increase the effect of its action.

As a martial artist, one could do a primary strike on the earth point of the pericardium channel (Pc 7), and then do the next strike on the front *mu* (alarm) point of the heart (Pc 7 and then Cv 14), in order to increase the damaging effect of the strike to the heart mu point. Thus, striking Pc 7 first increases the damage done to the heart when the Cv 14 point is struck. This is using the sheng cycle's mother/son theory, where the son is used to drain qi from the mother. The heart is the yin, or half the yin, of the fire element (pericardium is the other half). The pericardium is also seen as the protector of the heart, so damage here could increase damage to the heart.

Using an example from the KO cycle, one could strike to the metal point of the pericardium channel (Pc 5), then follow with a strike to front mu point of the liver (Liv 14). Here metal is acting to control the wood, and then further striking to a major point affecting the yin organ of the yin element adds insult to injury and results in dramatic results (perhaps liver shutdown). These are just examples of how these cycles might be used martially; there are lots of different combinations that could be used.

There is also a cycle called the reverse KO cycle (or counteracting or rebellious cycle). This is where one element rebels against its natural controller. This is an abnormal cycle and is symbolic of defiance. It may well be that at death the reverse KO cycle comes into play.

The format is as follows:

- Wood counteracts metal (by blunting it).
- Metal counteracts fire (by extinguishing it—cutting off its supply of oxygen).
- Fire counteracts water (by boiling it away if the fire is too vigorous).
- Water counteracts earth (by washing it away if the water is dammed to excess).
- Earth counteracts wood (by providing no foundation for its roots).

THE FIVE SHU POINTS

The five shu points are also called antique points, five element points, command points, and well points. They are all located below the elbows or the knees, since it is here that the energy in the channels is the most superficial, and the energy potential in the channel changes very rapidly in this region.

Thus, these points have a strong effect on the body when used either to heal or to disrupt an individual's energy patterns. These points can be used to disrupt qi flow in a channel in advance of a strike to a major knockout or death strike point, or to create a potentiality for healing by either boosting the qi in the channel or draining excess qi from the channel.

Jing Well Points

Jing well (*tsing*, *ting*, *ching*) points are wood on the yin channels and metal on the yang channels. They are located at the beginning or the end of the channel at the extremities of the fingers or toes. They are compared to the welling up of the water course. It is in the region of these points that the changeover of yin and yang qi occurs; the energy is very unstable here, so the use of these points is potentially very powerful.

These points dispel wind and heat. Bloodletting is most often applied to these points to clear heat (prick the point with a sterile needle and extract a few drops of blood). This is indicated for acute attacks of wind/heat or internal wind/heat that has caused loss of consciousness by drying the blood out of the vessels, as well as for heat in the blood that causes toxic skin conditions, bleeding nose, etc. These points also act on the muscle and divergent channels.

Ying Spring Points

Ying spring (*rong, yong, yung,* gushing) points are fire on the yin channels and water on the yang channels. These are located proximally to the jing well points, and it is here that the energy of the channel accelerates, like a spring bursting forth from the soil. They are also called acceleration-of-energy points and can be used to either increase or reduce the qi of the channel. They can be used to cool hot conditions and are usually reduced for this purpose by needling. They can be used with jing well points for draining excess qi from the channel and to treat excess in the muscle meridians. In shi conditions local points are used first, then distal points such as ying spring and/or jing well. Ying spring can also be used as good pep-up points.

Shu Stream Points

Shu stream (*yu*, transporting) points are earth on the yin channels and wood on the yang channels. These points are proximal to the ying spring points, and it is here that a pathogen that has entered a channel gets carried along, like a boat catching a stream. Their function is to eliminate pathogen energy from the channel, especially wind and damp, conditions, such as aching joints, etc. Here a reducing method is used; you can use ying spring and shu stream for this purpose (to treat arthritis that is seen as wind/damp bi syndrome in Chinese terms). On the yin channels the shu stream point is also the *yuan* source point, where the yuan qi (the physiologically active component of jing) resides and can be tapped to replenish and strengthen the vital energy of an organ or channel. Here a reinforcing method is applied.

Jing River Points

Jing river (*ching*, traversing) points are metal on the yin channels and fire on the yang channels. At these points the energy can be deviated out of the channel. They are used to treat cough and asthma (e.g., for cough from lung qi xu, you might use Kd 7 and Lu 9 or Sp 5, Lu 8, Kd 7, and Pc 5).

He Sea Points

He sea (*ho*, uniting) points are water on the yin channels and earth on the yang channels. At these points the qi penetrates deeper into the channel, passing through the internal organs, so these points can be used to stop pathogen energy from going deeper and also to regulate the associated organ. The arm 3 yang channels (Th, Si, and Co) share a more distant relationship with their internal organs than the other channels to their internal organs (*zhang/fu*), so there is an extra point for each on the leg, called a lower he sea point, which is used to treat the related organ (e.g., for the colon, St 37 is used as a lower he sea point).

Healing is the art of building/moving and balancing the body's qi, while martial arts is the art of stagnating, depleting, and scattering the body's qi. If you are going to learn to destroy, then also learn to build.

Bibliography

Beijing College of Traditional Medicine. 1980. *Essentials of Chinese Acupuncture, Beijing First Edition*. Beijing: Foreign Language Press.

Deshen, Wang. 1982. *Manual of International Standardization of Acupuncture Point Names*.

Kaptchuk, T.J. 1983. *Chinese Medicine: The Web That Has No Weaver*. London: Rider & Company.

Legge, David. 1991 to 1995. Seminars. Brisbane, Australia,

Matsumoto, Kiiko. 1995. Seminar. Sydney, Australia.

O'Connor, J., and D. Bensky, eds. 1981. *Acupuncture: A Comprehensive Text*. Seattle: Eastland Press.

Simpson, Wally. 1983 to 1986. Course notes from Acupuncture Colleges Australia/Brisbane.

Chapter 1

The Conceptor Vessel (Ren Mai)

The conceptor vessel/ren mai (Cv), along with the governor vessel/du mai (Gv), is one of the most important meridians for meditation and qigong. The "upper, heavenly circulation" travels up the Gv (yang) meridian and down the Cv (yin) meridian.

The Cv meridian dominates the yin of the whole body. Its function is to regulate the circulation of blood and qi in the yin meridians. Because of this, it is also known as "the sea of yin meridians." The three yin meridians of the hand and the three yin meridians of the foot all join at Cv 3.

This meridian originates in the uterus and is especially connected with conception; hence its name of "conceptor vessel." In fact, *ren* means conception or pregnancy, an obligation or responsibility. It can also mean to take in or to accept something in the front of the abdomen. In the healing area, it regulates the menstrual flow and dominates the reproductive system and the fetus. It regulates the qi circulation of the chest, promotes the function of the spleen and stomach, and generally strengthens the body. Points on the ren mai are usually indicated in diseases of the endocrinous and reproductive systems. They are used in the treatment of abdominal distension, vomiting, abdominal pain, diarrhea, coughing, asthma, sore throat, distension in the hypochondriac region, and disorders over the whole area of the path of the meridian. When this meridian is diseased, abnormal masses occur, such as hernia in males and splenomegaly (enlargement of the spleen) in females.

Just as the 12 main meridians are divided up into pairs, so, too, are four of the eight extra meridians. The ren mai's partner is the yin qiao mai. The ren mai is called the "master," while the yin qiao mai is called the "guest." The ren mai's is associated with the uterus, the eyes, and the lips. The coalescent points to this meridian are St 1, Gv 28, and Lu 7.

CV 1 (CONCEPTOR VESSEL POINT NO. 1)

Chinese name:

Huiyin (perineum).

Location:

In the center of the perineum, midway between the anus and the scrotum in men and midway between the anus and the commissura labiorum in females. *Hui* means crossing, and *yin* here is referring to the genitalia; the point is located in the space between the genitalia and the anus.

Connections:

Chong mai and governor vessel.

Direction:

Struck straight up into the center of the body.

Set-up point:

Liv 14 is also a point of the extra meridian yin wei mai. This point is used as a strike all by itself and does great damage. However, put it together with Cv 1 and you have a death point.

Damage:

Death or coma. Cv 1 is one of the very dangerous points if you can get at it! It is usually accessed using a toe strike upward between the anus and scrotum. If you can also use a taijiquan typical kick using the side of the foot on the big toe side (the edge), you can access Cv 1, chang mai, and Gv 1, a combination that you will have to be very serious about using! This is a point that is used in TCM for drowning, as it is the general luo, or connecting point of all eight extra meridians. It will supply jing qi to the body in the same way that a heavy strike to Kd 1 will in cases where the trauma has been so great that the heart has stopped and the body has no reserve of qi left to start it. In this case, the kidneys have stored qi for emergencies that can be accessed either by striking or bleeding Kd 1 or by applying pressure or needling 5 fen upward into Cv 1.

Antidote:

In the case where all three meridians have been attacked, there is not much hope of revival! However, you could try Kd 1 as above. Cv 1 will be too damaged to use anyway.

Healing:

Innervation is by the branch of the perineal nerve. Irrigation is by the branches of the perineal artery and vein.

Used for pruritus vulvae, irregular menstruation, pain and swelling of the anus, retention of urine, enuresis, seminal emission, mental disorders, revival from drowning, urethritis, and prostatitis.

This is a point of intersection with the governing channel/ chong (penetrating) channel. Its traditional function is to delay ejaculation in males if pressed during intercourse. (It can be used to cause arousal in both males and females prior to intercourse and, for females, during intercourse.)

To massage, press and hold, do rotation clockwise or counterclockwise for xu or shi conditions, or do light fingertip percussion.

Use with Gv 26, Pc 9, and Liv 3 for revival from drowning.

Use with Gv 1, Gv 20, St 36, Sp 3, Bl 30, Bl 57, Bl 25, Bl 24, Bl 23, Bl 20, Bl 17, and Bl 35 for hemorrhoids.

Use with Cv 2, Cv 3, Cv 4, Cv 5, Cv 6, Bl 28, Bl 25, Bl 26, Bl 22, St 28, Sp 9, Sp 6, St 36, Kd 3, Kd 7, Bl 18, and Liv 3 for prostatis.

Applications:

Take his right straight with your right palm as your left one comes underneath to take over (covered many times in the first volume of this book). Turn your waist to your right and come back instantly with a right elbow to Liv 14. This alone will probably kill him! Now, picking up where we left off in volume one, we begin with Figure 309. As shown, lift your right foot, turning it so that the big toe edge is uppermost, and strike straight up into Cv 1.

Figure 309

CV 2 (CONCEPTOR VESSEL POINT NO. 2)

Chinese name:

Qugu (crooked bone).

Location:

Qu means crooked, and *gu* means bone; the name refers to the location of the point on the midline of the abdomen, just above the symphysis pubis, 5 cun below the umbilicus, at the superior aspect of the symphysis pubis.

Connections:

Lower meeting point of Liv/Gb divergent meridians; liver meridian.

Direction:

Straight in to the top of the pubic bone.

Set-up point:

None.

Damage:

This strike is just as good as, if not better than, a strike to the groin. If struck hard enough, it can cause KO or even death. The potential dangers of this strike are sterility and cancer of the genital region.

Antidote:

See a doctor, either Chinese or Western. Treat Liv 6 with massage or needle.

Healing:

Innervation is by the branch of the iliohypogastric nerve.

Irrigation is by the branches of the inferior epigastric artery and the obturator artery.

Used for seminal emission, impotence, leukorrhea, retention of urine, hernia, irregular menstruation, prolapsed uterus, cystitis, orchitis, and prostitis.

Traditional functions: this is a point of intersection with the liver channel, so it influences that channel.

To massage, press and hold the point, do rotations clockwise or counterclockwise for xu or shi conditions, and press in slowly with both thumbs and release quickly, pulling the thumbs apart.

Use with Cv 3, Cv 4, Cv 5, Cv 6, Cv 9, St 28, Bl 28, Bl 25, Bl 24, Bl 23, Bl 22, Bl 18, Kd 3, Sp 9, and St 36 for retention of urine, prostitis, and cystitis.

Use with the extra point abdomen zigong, Gv 20, Cv 4, Cv 6, Cv 12, St 36, Cv 3, Sp 3, Sp 6, and Liv 3 for prolapsed uterus.

Use with Cv 3, Cv 4, Cv 6, Cv 9, Cv 12, St 25, St 26, St 28, St 29, Liv 4, Liv 3, and Sp 6 for lower abdomen pain from uterine fibroids, endometritis, etc.

Applications:

A straight front kick using the ball of the foot is indicated for this point.

CV 3 (CONCEPTOR VESSEL POINT NO. 3)

Chinese name:

Zhongji (middle summit or central pole).

Location:

On the anterior midline, 4 cun below the umbilicus, 1 cun above the upper border of the symphysis pubis. *Zhong* means center, and *ji* here means exactly; the point is exactly at the center of the body.

Connections:

Sp, Kd, and Liv.

Direction of strike:

Straight and slightly upward.

Damage:

This strike is one of the most damaging strikes to the genital area, as it will also affect the spleen, kidney, and liver. Immediately, the recipient will fall down with qi disruption, blood will probably flow from the penis, and he will probably die if medical attention is not sought. Later diseases are the same as for Cv 2.

Set-up point:

You could use either Sp 17 or Liv 13.

Antidote:

For the internal physical damage, see a doctor. Have an acupuncturist treat the bladder problems.

Healing:

Innervation is by the branch of the iliohypogastric nerve.

Irrigation is by the branches of the superficial epigastric and inferior epigastric arteries and veins.

Used for seminal emission, enuresis, retention of urine, frequency of micturition, pain in the lower abdomen, irregular menstruation, uterine bleeding, leukorrhea, prolapse of uterus, pain in the external genitalia, pruritis, impotence, premature ejaculation, female sterility, nephritis, urethritis, pelveoperitonitis, dysmenorrhea, and sciatica.

Traditional indications include irregular menstruation, lack of menstruation, excessive bleeding, vaginal discharge containing blood, itching in the vagina, vaginal pain, spontaneous loss of sperm, edema, frequent urination, and lack of urine.

Traditional functions are to regulate and promote the function of the uterus, regulate the lower jiao, eliminate damp heat, and assist the transforming functions of qi. When combined with Liv 5, it will eliminate liver fire. It is a mu point of the bladder, so will treat all pathologies of the bladder. As a point of intersection with the Sp/Kd/Liv Channels, it influences them.

Massage techniques are the same as for Cv 2.

See Cv 2 for treatment of retention of urine, prostitis, cystitis, uterine fibroids, endometritis, and so on.

Use with Cv 2, Kd 5, Cv 9, Sp 6, Gb 39, and Kd 7 for ascites from rheumatic heart disease.

Use with Kd 11, Sp 9, Gv 4, Bl 23, Kd 3, and Cv 4 for impotence, premature ejaculation, and spermatorrhea.

Use with Sp 6, Bl 23, Co 4, abdomen zigong (extra), Liv 3, and Liv 4 for irregular menstruation.

Applications:

He attacks with a straight right. You should slam his right neigwan with your right palm, reloading instantly the right elbow to attack to Sp 17 on his right side across his chest. Bring your knee upward into Cv 3.

CV 4 (CONCEPTOR VESSEL POINT NO. 4)

Chinese name:

Guanyuan (hinge at the source or gate origin).

Location:

On the midline of the abdomen, 3 cun below the umbilicus.

Connections:

Sp, Kd, and Liv.

Direction of strike:

Straight in and slightly upward. (Or downward or straight in, causing different reactions.)

Damage:

Cv 4 is one of the deadly points. It is not actually the tantien (an electrical area about 3 inches below the navel where the qi is said to be stored), but is situated just under it. The chong mai is an extra meridian that mostly travels through kidney points, so it is believed that the tantien (also called dantien by martial artists) is actually the kidneys. This is the area that we try to cultivate during qigong practice. We center the mind upon the tantien so that the qi will sink to the tantien. From there it is sent to all parts of the body so that we will have qi to do work. So, it is true to say that the qi comes from the tantien down to Kd 1 and then to all parts of the body—so if tantien is damaged, then death is not far off. A strike in the correct direction here, quite hard, will cause death from qi stoppage. Struck upward it will cause, in the immediate, extreme high blood pressure, fainting, and possible death. Struck downward it will cause extreme qi drainage with knockout. Struck straight in only, it will cause a slowing of the qi and, possibly, increasing sickness and death.

Set-up point:

Middle tantien point around Cv 14.

Antidote:

See a doctor of TCM. Or, if struck straight in, place the recipient in a coma position and rub the whole chest area downward and push up under the nose at Gv 26. If struck downward, massage Cv 14 and press Cv 1 lightly. If the point has been struck upward, tweak St 9 to bring the blood pressure down.

Cv 4 is a very dangerous point, however, and the antidotes may not work if too much damage has occurred.

Healing:

Innervation is by the anterior cutaneous nerve of the subcostal nerve. Irrigation is by the branches of the superficial and inferior artery and vein.

Used for seminal emission, enuresis, frequent micturition, retention of urine, irregular menstruation, dysmenorrhea, amenorrhea, leukorrhea, uterine bleeding, prolapsed uterus, postpartum hemorrhage, hernia, lower abdominal pain, diarrhea, flaccid apoplexy, dysentery, urinary tract infections, nephritis, pelveoperitonitis, impotence, and roundworm in the intestinal tract.

Traditional indications include abandoned stroke, general weakness, vaginal discharge, lack of menstruation, infertility, twisting pain below the navel, loss of sperm, hernia, blood in the urine, enuresis, blood in the stool, tidal fever accompanied by coughing up blood, emaciation and constant thirst, and dysentery.

This is a mu (alarm) point of the small intestine and a point of intersection with the spleen, kidney, and liver channels. Its traditional functions are to nourish and stabilize the kidneys, regulate the qi and restore yang, and regulate menstrual flow. *Guan* means storage, and *yuan* means primordial qi; this is the storage place of preheaven or ancestral qi, which results from the combination of our parents' sperm and ovum. This region is also called tantien by martial artists.

Massage techniques are the same as for Cv 2.

Use with Cv 6, Bl 23, Gv 4, Kd 3, Liv 3, Bl 18, Bl 24, Bl 26, Gb 24, Ht 7, and St 36 for impotence or loss of sperm. Use with Sp 9, Sp 6, Cv 3, Bl 28, Bl 25, Bl 18, Liv 3, and Liv 2 for urinary tract infections.

Use with Kd 1, Kd 2, Sp 9, Bl 67, Bl 66, Cv 3, Cv 2, Cv 6, Cv 5, and Bl 28 for acute pain in the lower abdomen and inability to urinate.

See Cv 2 for prolapsed uterus, uterine fibroids, and endometritis.

Use with St 36, Liv 3, Cv 6, Cv 12, Co 10, Kd 3, and Gv 20 for a general pickup.

Applications:

A rising heel kick to Cv 4, or a downward knee strike or a palm heel strike straight in.

CV 5 (CONCEPTOR VESSEL POINT NO. 5)

Chinese name:

Shimen (stone door).

Location:

On the midline of the abdomen, 2 cun below the umbilicus.

Connections:

None.

Direction of strike:

Straight in.

Damage:

Cv 5 is regarded as being the tantien point. Another name for it is ming men. Well, this point is a doozey! Even acupuncturists will avoid needling it if at all possible. In ancient texts on acupuncture, this point is said to shorten the patient's life or cause sterility in women! Any damage to this point will indeed shorten the recipient's life, as in dead right then. Trauma to this point will impede the internal communication needed for qi production, including the distribution of *yuan qi*, or ancestral qi, as well as blocking the smooth flow of qi between the three major points of Cv 3, 4, and 5. Cv 5 is the mu point for the triple warmer. It will impair a woman's reproduction and/or shorten life expectancy even if damaged lightly. Keep well clear of this part of the lower abdomen in training because even a light strike here could damage qi production and eventually shorten one's life.

Set-up point:

Middle or upper tantien, i.e., Cv 14 or yintang, respectively. *Yin* in this case means to dye, and *tang* means place. So yintang is a place of decoration. In China, people used to place some red paint onto this point, just between the eyebrows, to decorate themselves; hence the name of yintang.

Antidote:

None, really, for a hard strike, although you could try balancing the whole system using massage or needling techniques.

Healing:

Used for uterine bleeding, leukorrhea, amenorrhea, postpartum hemorrhage, hernia, abdominal pain, diarrhea, retention of urine, enuresis, edema, and mastitis.

Traditional functions: this is a mu point of the triple heater (sanjiao), so it can help regulate water passage. Shi means stone, and men means door; this point is indicated for treating lumps in the lower abdomen (lumps are often hard like stones). Massage techniques are the same as for Cv 2.

Use with St 28, Kd 6, Sp 9, Sp 4, Liv 4, St 25, Bl 22, Bl 23, Bl 28, Bl 23, Bl 20, St 40, Cv 2, Cv 3, Cv 4, and Cv 9 for fluid retention in the lower abdomen, edema, retention of urine, and enuresis.

Use with Cv 17, Liv 3, Liv 14, St 18, St 15, Sp 18, Kd 22, Kd 23, Si 1, Si 3, St 40, St 44, St 45, Bl 17, Bl 18, and Bl 22 for mastitis.

Applications:

A toe kick straight in to Cv 6 is all that is needed. You will not hurt your toes; this area is very soft.

CV 6 (CONCEPTOR VESSEL POINT NO. 6)

Chinese name:

Qihai (sea of qi).

Location:

On the midline of the abdomen, 1.5 cun below the umbilicus or halfway between Cv 7 and Cv 5.

Connections:

None.

Direction of strike:

Straight in.

Damage:

Again, this is a very dangerous point. You could strike Cv 5 and Cv 6 together for a devastating result. It is said in ancient dim-mak texts that there is no return from this double strike! When struck, the qi circulation overall will be upset or stopped, resulting in either instant or delayed death! When a severe strike has occurred to this point, it takes around three days for the qi to slow down and stop flowing. Or if the strike is very hard, it means instant death. Even lighter strikes will impair the kidney function for life, causing the quality of life to be diminished.

Set-up point:

Cv 14 or yintang.

Antidote:

None, although you could have an acupuncturist needle this point 8 fen perpendicular. This will help to strengthen the yuan qi to all the organs, especially to the kidneys.

Healing:

Innervation and irrigation are the same as for Cv 5.

Use for uterine bleeding, leukorrhea, irregular menstruation, postpartum hemorrhage, hernia, enuresis, abdominal pain, diarrhea, constipation, neurasthenia, abdominal distention, dysmenorrhea, intestinal paralysis, incontinence, polyuria, urinary retention, spermatorrhea, and impotence.

Traditional indications include vaginal discharge with blood, irregular menstruation, excessive bleeding, infertility, colic, incontinence among children, heat stroke (or exhaustion), and abandoned stroke.

Qi in this instance means primary qi, and *hai* means sea; this is the sea of the primary qi of the whole body. Its traditional functions are to regulate qi circulation, tonify weakness, strengthen deficient kidneys, and dispel damp.

Massage techniques are the same as for Cv 2.

Use with Cv 3, Cv 4, Sp 6, Liv 3, Liv 4, Sp 9, St 36, St 27, Bl 17, Bl 18, St 28, St 29, St 26, St 25, Kd 11, Kd 12, Kd 13, Kd 14, Kd 15, and Kd 16 for dysmenorrhea and irregular menstruation.

Add Sp 10 and Co 4 for excessive bleeding.

Add Gb 26, Bl 20, and Bl 23 for leukorrhea.

Add Bl 23, Bl 20, Bl 26, Gv 4, and Gv 20 for impotence.

Applications:

The same as for Cv 5, although you could use the knee because it is slightly higher, allowing for a set-up strike to either Cv 14 or yintang prior to the knee strike.

CV 7 (CONCEPTOR VESSEL POINT NO. 7)

Chinese name:

Yinjiao (yin's junction).

Location:

On the midline of the abdomen, 1 cun below the umbilicus.

Connections:

Pericardium, triple heater, and chong mai.

Direction of strike:

Straight in.

Damage:

This point is also dangerous, but not as dangerous as the last two. It is getting a little higher up, and although it is not greatly protected, it is relative to Cv 5 and 6. A strike here—should you not also get Cv 5 and 6 with the same strike—will cause KO; if the strike is hard enough it could cause death from kidney failure.

Set-up point:

Same as for Cv 6.

Antidote:

You could use any of the kidney yang boosters, such as Kd 1, or the same point, Cv 7, using massage or needle methods.

Healing:

Innervation is by the anterior cutaneous branch of the 10th intercostal nerve. Irrigation is the same as for Cv 3.

Used for uterine bleeding, leukorrhea, irregular menstruation, pruritis vulvae, abdominal pain around the umbilicus, hernia, postpartum hemorrhage, edema, and prolapsed uterus.

Yin is as in yin/yang, and *jiao* means crossing. This point's traditional functions are as the crossing point of the chong (penetrating) mai and the kidney channel.

Massage techniques are the same as for Cv 2.

Use with St 25, Liv 4, Liv 8, Liv 3, Liv 2, Cv 4, Cv 6, Bl 18, Bl 19, Bl 17, Bl 20, Bl 22, Bl 23, Bl 25, Bl 26, Sp 9, and Sp 6 for dysmenorrhea.

Use with Ht 1, Sp 7, Pc 6, Ht 7, Bl 14, Bl 15, Bl 17, Bl 18, Cv 17, Liv 14, Liv 3, Liv 4, Cv 14, and St 36 for angina.

Use with Bl 23, Bl 18, Bl 20, Sp 6, St 36, Liv 3, Cv 4, Cv 6, Bl 17, Sp 10, St 30, Sp 8, Kd 5, Cv

Figure 310

Figure 311

3, and Gb 21 for amenorrhea.

Applications:

A back turning kick works well to this point (but not a back spinning kick because this is too slow). You might take his straight right attack with your left palm as you step in, turning your left foot to your right (fig. 310). Now turn your whole body so that your right foot is thrust backward at great speed and power into Cv 7 (fig. 311).

CV 8 (CONCEPTOR VESSEL POINT NO. 8)

Chinese name:

Qizhong (middle of navel) or shenque (spirit palace gate).

Location:

In the middle of the umbilicus.

Connections:

None.

Direction of strike:

Straight in to the navel.

Damage:

The navel is not well protected. Although it is higher up on the stomach than the previous Cv points, there is a direct link to the internal through this point. The area all around Cv 8 is well protected by muscle, but what's right in the middle is not. So it is easy to inflict damage at this point. A strike here causes spleen damage as well as physical stomach damage. It will cause much yang qi to spread out all over the torso and up into the head, resulting in knockout or death if it is a hard strike. This is also a very dangerous point. Acupuncturists are warned not to needle this point, only to use moxa on it to warm the yang qi of the body (and even then the moxa is burnt over salt or ginger).

Figure 312

Set-up point:

Cv 17 downward.

Antidote:

For the KO, depending upon how serious it is, use Gb 20, squeezing upward. For more serious KO or death use CPR.

Healing:

Irrigation is by the inferior epigastric artery and vein.

Used for flaccid-type apoplexy, borborgymus, abdominal pain, unchecked diarrhea, prolapsed rectum, acute and chronic enteritis, intestinal tuberculosis, shock from intestinal adhesions, and edema.

Traditional indications include apoplexy, heat stroke (or exhaustion), loss of consciousness, intestinal noises and pain, continuous diarrhea, prolapsed anus, and simultaneous vomiting and diarrhea.

Shen means spirit, and *que* here means palace gate. Shenque's traditional function is as an important passage for the circulation of fetal qi and xue, or blood. Therefore, it is considered to be like a palace gate of the qi (spirit). It also warms and stabilizes the yang and strengthens the transporting function of the spleen and stomach.

To massage, you can press it with the heel of the palm, cup it, or use moxa on this point.

To treat unchecked diarrhea, place salt in the navel and a thin slice of ginger over the top, then burn medium-sized cones of loose punk moxa over the point.

Use with St 25, Cv 13, Pc 6, St 36, Sp 4, St 40, Co 4, Bl 25, Bl 20, and Bl 22 for acute gastritis.

Use with Cv 9, Cv 7, Cv 6, St 25, Kd 16, Liv 4, Liv 3, St 36, Sp 4, Sp 5, Sp 9, Gb 26, and Gv 4 for pain around the umbilicus.

Applications:

He might attack with a straight right from behind. Swing around and, using your right palm, slam his forearm. Hook his forearm over to your left, thus opening him up as you step in with a right palm strike to Cv 17 downward, followed instantly with a pumping left spear finger attack to Cv 8 (fig. 312).

CV 9 (CONCEPTOR VESSEL POINT NO. 9)

Chinese name:

Shuifen (water part).

Location:

On the midline of the abdomen, 1 cun above the umbilicus.

Connections:

Lungs.

Direction of strike:

Straight in.

Damage:

This removes power by attacking the lungs, spleen, and kidneys. There is not much physical damage here; it is all electrical since this point is fairly well protected. The use of "iron shirt" training will also enhance the protection. Iron shirt qigong is a type of protective qigong that builds up a sort of "barrel" of muscle around the abdomen. There are many different types of iron shirt; however, there is only one that really works to protect the abdomen—that which comes from the internal martial arts. There are many instructors out there teaching the internal martial arts, but most teach hard-style iron shirt. Some have even been known to give people hernia ·from this extremely hard practice. So be careful when seeking out an iron shirt teacher. Look to see whether that teacher is teaching soft-style qigong, with no heavy breathing, tensing of anus or stomach muscles, clenching of fists, etc. If you see him going red in the face, then walk out! Iron shirt training is also only ever learned from actual training, i.e., having someone strike you and learning not to greatly tense the muscles. This will help in the building up of the "barrel" for protection.

Set-up point:

Lu 5.

Antidote:

To bring back the power, place pressure onto Lu 1, using the thumb.

Healing:

Innervation is by the anterior cutaneous branches of the eighth and ninth intercostal nerves. Irrigation is the same as for Cv 8. Used for borborygmus, abdominal pain, edema, ascites, vomiting, diarrhea, and nephritis.

Traditional functions: *shui* means water, and *fen* means separation; this point corresponds internally to the small intestine, where water and food separate into turbid and clear.

Massage techniques are the same as for Cv 2.

Use with Cv 2, Cv 3, Cv 4, Cv 5, Cv 6, Cv 7, St 28, St 40, Sp 9, St 25, Cv 12, Kd 6, Bl 28, Bl 23, Bl 22, Bl 20, Bl 39, St 36, Sp 4, and Sp 6 for fluid retention, ascites, diarrhea, and borborygmus.

Use with Cv 12, St 25, Liv 13, Cv 4, Cv 6, Bl 20, Bl 21, Bl 22, Bl 25, St 36, Liv 3, Sp 3, Sp 4, Sp 5, and Sp 9 for abdominal pain.

Use with Pc 6, St 36, Cv 12, St 25, Liv 3, Bl 20, Bl 21, Bl 19, Bl 18, Sp 3, and Liv 13 for vomiting.

Applications:

Strike his right hook with the back of your right palm at Lu 5. Rebound your right elbow into Cv 9.

CV 10 (CONCEPTOR VESSEL POINT NO. 10)

Chinese name:

Xiawan (lower cavity).

Location:

Xia means inferior, and wan means stomach; the point is at the inferior portion of the stomach, on the midline of the abdomen, 2 cun above the umbilicus.

Connections:

Spleen.

Direction of strike:

Straight in and slightly upward.

Damage:

This point, when struck along with Cv 12 and 13, will damage the production of qi, slow it down, and eventually stop its flow, causing death. So, although death is not necessarily immediate, it will slowly come after a bout of ill health that gradually gets worse.

None, although you can strike to Cv 12 and 13 at almost the same time. This is a three-point strike, causing death.

Antidote:

The same points will have to be needled by an acupuncturist to improve the flow and production of qi.

Your own qigong will also help this, if you are not dead!

Healing:

Innervation is by the anterior cutaneous branch of the eighth intercostal nerve. Irrigation is the same as for Cv 8.

Used for gastric pain, abdominal distension, dysentery, borborygmus, vomiting, undigested food in stool, indigestion, prolapsed stomach, and diarrhea.

As a crossing point of the spleen channel, this point's traditional function is to influence that channel. Massage techniques are the same as for Cv 2.

Use with Cv 12, Cv 9, St 25, Liv 13, Cv 14, Bl 20, Bl 21, Bl 18,

Bl 25, Bl 23, St 36, Kd 3, Liv 3, Cv 4, Cv 6, St 28, and Sp 9 for diarrhea, dysentery, and undigested food in the stool; add Sp 10, Co 4, Cv 11, and Bl 17 if there is bloody dysentery.

Add to formula for vomiting listed under Cv 9.

Use with formula for abdominal pain listed under Cv 9.

Use with Gv 20, Cv 4, Cv 6, Cv 12, *weishangxue* (an extra point), St 36, Sp 3, Bl 21, Bl 20, Bl 18, Bl 17, and Pc 6 for prolapsed stomach.

Applications:

Simply slam the three points with your palms.

CV 11 (CONCEPTOR VESSEL POINT NO. 11)

Chinese name:

Jianli (establish measure).

Location:

On the midline of the abdomen, 3 cun above the umbilicus.

Connections:

None.

Direction of strike:

Straight in.

Damage:

This point in particular is well protected. Striking here, catching the opponent unaware, however, will cause great internal damage with qi drainage, causing KO.

Set-up point:

Neigwan.

Antidote:

Gb 20. See a doctor for the internal damage.

Healing:

Innervation is by the anterior cutaneous branch of the eighth intercostal nerve. Irrigation is by the branches of the superior and inferior epigastric arteries.

Used for gastric pain, vomiting, anorexia, abdominal distension, edema, acute and chronic gastritis, angina pectoris, ascites, intestinal noises, and abdominal pain.

Jian here means establishing; *li* means interior; the point is in the epigastric region, and its traditional function is to aid in establishing the qi of the middle jiao, or heater.

Massage techniques are the same as for Cv 2.

Use with Cv 17, Cv 16, Cv 15, Cv 14, Cv 13, Cv 12, Cv 9, Cv 7, Cv 6, Cv 5, Cv 4, Cv 3, Cv 2, St 25, St 21, St 36, Liv 3, Liv 4, Sp 9, Sp 4, Liv 13, Bl 25, Bl 26, Bl 20, Bl 21, and Bl 18 for abdominal distension and pain, borborygmus, gastric pain, and ascites.

Use with Pc 6, Bl 17, Bl 43, Bl 15, Bl 14, Bl 18, Bl 19, Cv 17, Liv 14, Liv 3, St 36, Gb 34, Ht 7, and Sp 6 for angina.

Applications:

Obvious.

CV 12 (CONCEPTOR VESSEL POINT NO. 12)

Chinese name:

Zhongwan (middle cavity).

Location:

On the midline of the abdomen, 4 cun above the umbilicus. *Zhong* means middle, and *wan* means stomach; the point is in the middle of the stomach.

Connections:

Lung, pericardium, small intestine, triple heater, and stomach.

Direction of strike:

Slightly upward.

Damage:

See the damage for Cv 10. Plus, this point will cause vomiting and even diarrhea. It has so many connections that any strike here is dangerous. It is the mu point of the stomach, a special meeting point of the fu (hollow or yang organs), and the meeting point of middle and triple heaters. A strike here will cause disharmony in the yin and yang or earth and disharmony with earth's relationship to metal. It will also cause emotional problems resulting in physical disorders, such as obesity. So a strike to this point, although causing immediate damage, will also cause latent damage.

Set-up point:

Th points are good for this strike, although it is difficult to strike to Th 8, for instance, because you want to get at the centerline. So I would suggest a hard strike to neigwan, since this works just as well in setting up Cv 12.

Antidote:

Neigwan, massaged or needled; qi balancing qigong. There is much that has to be done when this point is struck, however, so it is best to see a TCM doctor and explain what has happened.

Healing:

Innervation is by the anterior cutaneous branch of the seventh intercostal nerve. Irrigation is by the superior epigastric artery and vein.

Used for gastric pain, abdominal distension, regurgitation, vomiting, diarrhea, dysentery, undigested food in stool, acute or chronic gastritis, gastric ulcers, prolapsed stomach, acute intestinal obstruction, constipation, hypertension, neurasthenia, indigestion, and mental illness.

Traditional indications include pain in the stomach cavity, vomiting food long after ingestion, sour taste upon swallowing, indigestion, lack of appetite, abdominal pain or distension, dysentery, constipation, spitting blood that's related to consumptive disease, madness, and jaundice.

As a mu point of the stomach, one of its traditional functions is to treat all conditions of this organ. As a crossing point of the small intestine, it also regulates the stomach qi, tonifies the spleen, relieves retention of food, eliminates damp, and transforms and suppresses rebellious stomach qi. As a point of intersection with the Si, Th, and St channels, it is an influential point of the fu organs (St, Si, Th, Bl, Gb, and Co), so it can have an effect on all of these organs.

Massage techniques are the same as for Cv 2.

Use with Pc 6, St 21, Liv 13, Liv 3, Cv 9, St 25, St 36, Sp 4, and Co 4 for nausea and vomiting.

Use with St 36, Cv 4, Cv 6, Cv 17, Kd 3, Liv 3, Sp 3, Sp 6, Co 4, Th 4, and Gv 20 to lift the energy of the body.

Use with Liv 13, St 25, St 21, Cv 13, Cv 14, St 36, St 40, Sp 9, Co 4, Co 11, Pc 6, Bl 20, Bl 25, Bl 21, and Bl 18 to remove food stagnation causing pain and discomfort.

Use with Kd 1, Gv 20, the extra point yintang, Liv 3, Pc 6, Ht 7, St 36, Sp 3, Kd 16, and St 40 for mental illness.

Applications:

Same as for the previous point. Or you could simply use a back heel kick or a front toe kick.

CV 13 (CONCEPTOR VESSEL POINT NO. 13)

Chinese name:
Shangwan (upper cavity).

Location:
Shang means superior, and *wan* means stomach; the point is at the upper portion of the stomach, on the midline of the abdomen, 5 cun above the umbilicus.

Connections:
Lung, stomach, and small intestine.

Direction of strike:
Slightly upward.

Damage:
See Cv 10 and 12. Plus, this strike will also affect the heart and lungs, draining qi and causing great weakness.

Set-up point:
Lu 5.

Antidote:
Apply pressure to Si 11 in the middle of the scapular. This is usually a very sore point even in healthy people. However, if Cv 13 has been struck, you will hardly be able to touch it.

Healing:
Innervation and irrigation are the same as for Cv 12.

Use for gastric pain, regurgitation, vomiting, epilepsy, dilated stomach, stomach spasms, cardiac spasms, and acute and chronic gastritis.

Traditional indications include fever with no sweating, irritable and feverish heart, chest pain, distension of the abdomen, excessive salivation, and jaundice.

As a point of intersection with the stomach and small intestine channels, its traditional function is to influence those channels.

Massage techniques are the same as for Cv 2.

Use with Cv 12, St 21, St 36, Pc 6, Liv 13, Liv 3, St 25, Co 4, Cv 4, Cv 6, Cv 9, Bl 25, Bl 20, Bl 21, Bl 19, Bl 18, and Bl 17 for food stagnation, nausea, and so on.

Use with Pc 6, Cv 17, Cv 14, Sp 4, St 36, and Liv 3 for cardiac spasm.

Use with Pc 6, Cv 12, St 36, St 44, St 45, Sp 5, Sp 9, Sp 4, Liv 3, Bl 20, Bl 21, Bl 18, Bl 17, Bl 19, and Co 4 for acute or chronic gastritis.

Applications:
This point is struck slightly upward using a smaller weapon such as a one-knuckle punch. If you can strike hard enough to get at Cv 14, then this is a death strike in the most extreme.

CV 14 (CONCEPTOR VESSEL POINT NO. 14)

Chinese name:
Juque (great palace or shrine).

Location:
On the midline of the abdomen, 6 cun above the umbilicus or 1 cun below the xiphoid process of the sternum.

Connections:
None.

Direction of strike:
Straight in.

Damage:
This is one of the most dangerous points. People have been known to die when struck, for instance, with a cricket ball (or a baseball) right on the point at noon. This point stops the heart because it is

the heart mu point. A strike here can also cause mental illness and disharmony between the shen and the mind. A person receiving a strike here can actually die from a coughing/vomiting attack!

Set-up point:
Neigwan, although this point really doesn't need a set-up point.

Antidote:
None.

Healing:
Innervation and irrigation are the same as for Cv 12.

Used for pain in the cardiac region and chest, regurgitation, difficulty swallowing, nausea, vomiting, mental disorders, epilepsy, palpitations, angina pectoris, stomachache, hiccups, roundworm in the bile duct, and chronic hepatitis.

Traditional indications include coughing due to rebellious rising of qi, palpitations from fright, vomiting long after the ingestion of food, jaundice, chest pain related to roundworm, and epigastric pain.

Traditional function is to calm the spirit (shen) and regulate the qi, pacify the stomach, and benefit the diaphragm. Also, *ju* here means great, and *que* means palace gate; this is the mu point of the heart channel, like a door to the qi of the heart, so it can treat all problems of the heart and its channel.

Massage techniques are the same as for Cv 2.

Use with Bl 15, Bl 14, Bl 17, Bl 18, Pc 4, Pc 6, Ht 5, Ht 7, St 36, Liv 3, Liv 14, Co 4, and Cv 17 for angina pectoris.

Use with Cv 12, St 21, St 36, St 25, Liv 13, Liv 3, Bl 20, Bl 21, Bl 19, Bl 18, Bl 17, Pc 6, Co 4, and Co 10 for food stagnation, vomiting, nausea, etc.

Use with Th 10, Pc 6, Pc 3, Ht 7, Kd 1, Gv 20, Bl 15, Bl 17, Bl 18, Bl 20, Bl 25, St 25, St 36, Liv 3, Sp 6, Sp 3, St 40, Sp 9, yintang, Cv 17, Lu 1, and Lu 7 for mental instability.

Applications:
Again, a one-knuckle punch aimed slightly upward. This one needs to be a smaller weapon, although the larger ones such as a palm strike will also work since the point is just so sensitive.

CV 15 (CONCEPTOR VESSEL POINT NO. 15)

Chinese name:
Jiuwei (wild pigeon's tail).

Location:
Jiu means turtle dove, and *wei* means tail; this point is below the xiphoid process of the sternum, which resembles a turtledove's tail. It is 0.5 cun below the xiphoid process of the sternum, or 7 cun above the umbilicus. Locate the point in the supine position with the arms uplifted.

Connections:
None.

Direction of strike:
Straight in and slightly upward.

Damage:
This point is also a heart stopper, but it is not as dangerous as Cv 14. It will also cause mental illness, along with a peculiar side effect of itching skin that cannot be cured using normal Western medicine.

Set-up point:
Neigwan.

Antidote:
Have an acupuncturist needle Cv 16 slightly downward to cure the itching and mental illness. (These Cv points are just so complicated, however, that a complete TCM examination is suggested when any of them have been struck.)

Healing:

Innervation and irrigation are the same as for Cv 12.

Use for pain in the cardiac region and chest, regurgitation, mental disorders, epilepsy, asthma, hiccups, and angina pectoris.

As a luo point of the Cv channel, its traditional functions are to affect all the yin connecting channels of the abdomen.

Massage techniques are the same as for Cv 2 (be careful here, as too much pressure could damage or break the xiphoid process).

Use with the formula for angina pectoris listed under Cv 14.

Use with Lu 1, Lu 5, Lu 7, Co 4, Pc 6, dingchuan (an extra point), Cv 22, Liv 14, Liv 3, St 36, St 40, Bl 43, Bl 12, Bl 13, Bl 17, Bl 18, Cv 17, and Cv 12 for asthma.

Add to formula for mental disorders listed under Cv 14.

Use with Bl 17, Bl 18, Cv 14, Cv 22, Pc 6, Cv 12, Cv 17, St 36, Liv 2, St 44, Cv 4, Cv 6, St 25, and Gb 21 for hiccups.

Applications:

The same as for Cv 14.

CV 16 (CONCEPTOR VESSEL POINT NO. 16)

Chinese name:

Zhongting (middle hall or courtyard).

Location:

Zhong means middle, and *ting* means hall or courtyard; this point is below the heart like a courtyard in front of the palace. It is on the middle of the sternum, level with the fifth intercostal space, or 1.6 cun below Cv 17.

Connections:

None.

Direction of strike:

Slightly downward.

Damage:

This point will also do great damage because it is between the xiphoid process and the sternum and is not very well protected. Physical damage is incurred, as well as internal damage. Vomiting and coughing attacks will occur. A strike here will cause KO—and death if it is very hard.

Set-up point:

Striking to both forearms at neigwan is an excellent set-up strike for this point.

Antidote:

None.

Healing:

Innervation is by the anterior cutaneous branch of the sixth intercostal nerve. Irrigation is by the perforating branches of the internal mammary artery and vein.

Used for sensation of fullness in the chest, difficulty swallowing, asthma, and vomiting.

Traditional functions are to stop infantile vomiting, ease hypochondriac pain, and increase appetite.

Massage techniques are the same as for Cv 2, plus fingertip percussion.

Use with the formula for asthma listed under Cv 15.

Use with Cv 12, Pc 6, Liv 3, St 44, St 40, Gb 20, Bl 18, Cv 22, Cv 14, Cv 12, St 21, Liv 14, Liv 13, Liv 3, Pc 6, Co 4, St 36, Gb 21, Bl 20, Bl 17, Bl 18, Bl 19, Bl 21, Bl 25, and St 25 for difficulty swallowing.

Applications:

He attacks with both hands. You use fa-jing energy to strike first to his right wrist at Pc 6 and then immediately to his left Pc 6 before coming straight in to Cv 16 with your elbow or one-knuckle punch. This method is much the same as that of the first of the original dim-mak forms.

CV 17 (CONCEPTOR VESSEL POINT NO. 17)

Chinese name:

Shanzhong or tanzhong (penetrating odor).

Location:

On the midline of the sternum, between the nipples, level with the fourth intercostal space. *Tan* means exposure, and *zhong* means middle; the point is located at the exposed middle part of the chest, called *tanzhong* in ancient times.

Connections:

Kidney, small intestine, pericardium, and triple heater.

Direction of strike:

Downward is the only way to strike this point.

Damage:

Cv 17 is another of the very dangerous strikes. (In fact, the Cv meridian for a dim-mak expert is like a kid in a candy factory.) This point traditionally drains energy from the seat of power, or the diaphragm. Striking this point downward causes KO at least and death at most. The recipient will fall down from lack of power. A warning comes with this point for those who would play around with it: never use this point on anyone under the age of 25! The sternum cartilage has not yet hardened and can be broken easily in younger people. This point has many properties. It is the mu point of the pericardium; hence, it will attack the heart. It is a meeting point of shao yin (heart and kidney), a sea of energy point with Bl 10 and St 9, and a meeting point of upper and middle heaters. It will deregulate the flow of qi throughout the system and totally destroy the relationship and balance between water and fire within the system.

Set-up point:

Neigwan and a slicing blow upward into the face using the tips of the fingers. This is a method from bagwazhang called the eagle technique and is the 11th deadly kata covered in my book *Dim-Mak's 12 Most Deadly Katas.* Another excellent set-up point is Bl 10, and this can be got at from a grappling-type situation. A little strike at the back of the neck will cause the attacker to drop, but just before he does, the strike to Cv 17 will finish him.

Antidote:

Have an acupuncturist apply two cones of moxa to the point.

Healing:

Innervation is by the anterior cutaneous branch of the fourth intercostal nerve. Irrigation is by the anterior perforating branches of the internal thoracic artery and vein.

Used for asthma, hiccups, pain in the chest, lactation deficiency, bronchitis, mastitis, and intercostal neuralgia.

Traditional indications include wheezing, panting, spitting and coughing blood, difficulty or inability to swallow food (as a result of constriction and dryness in the esophagus), tumors in the neck, lung abscess, and chest pain.

As a mu point of the pericardium, its traditional functions are to regulate the qi circulation, subdue ascending qi of the stomach, dispel fullness of the chest, soothe the diaphragm, clear the lungs, and resolve phlegm. It is also a meeting point of qi: it is a primary point for qi of the chest, ancestral qi gathers here, and sanjiao mai (Th channel) crosses the Cv meridian here. It calms the shen, or spirit.

Massage techniques are the same as for Cv 16. You can also use loose fist to percuss this point, as long as you don't go too hard. Use with Si 1, St 36, Bl 18, Bl 20, St 18, Liv 3, Pc 6, and Ht 7 for insufficient lactation.

See Cv 15 for treatment of asthma.

See formula listed under Cv 14 for angina.

Use with Liv 14, St 15, St 18, Sp 18, Si 1, Gb 21, St 36, Liv 3, Pc 6, Sp 6, Kd 6, Bl 22, Bl 17, Bl 18, Bl 20, and Bl 19 for mastitis.

Applications:

1) Strike his right neigwan with the back of your right palm as he attacks. Your right palm now turns to palm facing down, and the fingers flick violently upward, attacking the front of his face. Then the right palm slams downward into Cv 17.

2) From a grappling situation (and remember that these techniques are illegal in any of the recent spate of Ultimate Fighting Championships), strike using the reverse knife edge of one of your palms to the back of his neck at Bl 10. This will cause KO. Then, strike downward using your elbow to Cv 17.

CV 18 (CONCEPTOR VESSEL POINT NO. 18)

Chinese name:

Yutang (jade court).

Location:

On the midline of the sternum, level with the third intercostal space, 1.6 cun above Cv 17.

Connections:

None.

Direction of strike:

Slightly downward.

Damage:

This point is very well protected and is a point that I would not use in a tight situation. However, it will do damage if struck hard enough. It produces coughing fits, and local pain and qi drainage are also apparent (it must be struck with a smaller weapon to do any qi damage).

Set-up point:

None.

Antidote:

For local pain or tendon damage, see a doctor.

Healing:

Innervation is by the anterior cutaneous branch of the third intercostal nerve. Irrigation is the same as for Cv 16.

Use for cough, asthma, pain in the chest, bronchitis, vomiting, emphysema, and intercostal neuralgia.

The point is located over the site of the heart, and jade is thought to be of great value, as is the heart, so the point is thought of as a jade palace. Its traditional function is to send energy down, countering rebellious qi.

Massage techniques are the same as for Cv 17.

Use with the formula for asthma listed under Cv 15.

Use with Bl 12, Bl 13, Bl 43, Bl 17, Bl 18, Bl 20, Cv 17, Cv 12, Lu 1, Lu 7, Lu 5, Co 4, Co 11, St 40, St 36, Liv 14, Liv 13, Liv 3, Gv 10, and Gv 12 for emphysema.

Use with Pc 6, St 36, Sp 4, Sp 3, Liv 3, Liv 2, Liv 13, Cv 12, St 21, Cv 14, and Co 4 for vomiting.

See the formula listed under Cv 14 for chest pain and angina.

Applications:

The same as for Cv 17.

CV 19 (CONCEPTOR VESSEL POINT NO. 19)

Chinese name:

Chest zigong (purple palace).

Location:

On the midline of the sternum, level with the second intercostal space, 1.6 cun above Cv 18.

Connections:

None.

Direction of strike:

Straight in.

Damage:

This point produces much the same as Cv 18, only more local pain is felt with more qi drainage. It can be used in situations where the attacker has to be controlled, as in the case of a doorman or bouncer. A quick shot using a one-knuckle punch ("I only hit him in the chest, officer!"), and he will be putty in your hands, coughing and spluttering. Then use one finger to Th 17 while the other hand controls the head for extra pressure, and take him out, no worries.

Set-up point:

A slap across the neck using the flat of the palm cupped to completely confuse the system, followed by the strike to Cv 19.

Antidote:

Release the pressure to Th 17 and he will be OK (hopefully!).

Healing:

Innervation is by the anterior cutaneous branch of the second intercostal nerve. Irrigation is the same as for Cv 16.

Used for cough, asthma, pain in the chest, bronchiectasis, and pulmonary tuberculosis.

Traditional functions: *Zi* means purple, and *gong* here means palace; zigong is the name of a star, and here it refers to the emperor's palace. It is called zigong because it functions as the officer of the heart, which is the monarch.

Massage techniques are the same as for Cv 17.

For asthma, use with the formula listed under Cv 15, plus points Cv 17, Cv 18, Cv 20, and Cv 21.

Use with Cv 18, Cv 17, Cv 15, Cv 14, Liv 14, Liv 3, Liv 13, Cv 12, Bl 14, Bl 15, Bl 43, Bl 17, Bl 18, and Gb 24 for chest pain.

Applications:

He comes at you with either both or one hand. Slam his neigwan with either your right or left back palm, and rebound into his neck using a cupped hand. This will put a percussive strike into his neck, causing KO in itself of great confusion. Follow this with the strike using a one-knuckle punch to Cv 19.

CV 20 (CONCEPTOR VESSEL POINT NO. 20)

Chinese name:

Huagai (lustrous cover).

Location:

On the midline of the sternum, at the level of the first intercostal space or 1 cun below Cv 21. *Hua* here means magnificent, and *gai* means umbrella; this point name refers to the emperor's umbrella. The location of the point corresponds to the lung, which is like an umbrella above the heart.

Connections:

None.

Direction of strike:

Same as for Cv 19, although you could glance upward into Cv 22, which will cause death. I see no reason to strike this point; it is close to Cv 22, which is much more dangerous.

Damage:

Same as for Cv 19.

Set-up point:

Same as for Cv 19.

Antidote:

Same as for Cv 19.

Healing:

Innervation is by the anterior cutaneous branch of the first intercostal nerve. Irrigation is the same as for Cv 16.

Use for asthma, cough, chest pain, bronchitis, intercostal neuralgia, and pharyngitis.

Traditional function is to promote the descending and dispersing function of the lungs, send qi down, and disperse accumulation in the chest.

Massage techniques are the same as for Cv 17.

Use with Bl 12, Bl 13, Bl 43, Bl 17, Bl 18, Bl 20, Bl 23, Cv 12, Cv 17, Cv 18, Cv 19, Cv 22, Cv 21, Lu 1, Lu 7, St 36, St 40, Liv 14, Liv 13, Liv 3, Sp 4, and Pc 6 for bronchial asthma.

Use with Lu 6, Bl 13, Gv 14, St 36, Sp 4, Lu 9, Lu 1, Kd 3, Kd 6, St 25, Ht 7, Ht 6, Cv 12, Sp 6, Bl 23, Cv 4, Cv 17, Bl 20, Bl 17, Bl 18, and Bl 43 for pulmonary tuberculosis.

For intercostal neuralgia, use with jiaji points corresponding to the region, Liv 14, Gb 24, Cv 17, Cv 18, Sp 21, Liv 2, Liv 3, Gb 43, Gb 44, Gb 34, Bl 17, Bl 18, Bl 19, Bl 20, Bl 21, Pc 7, and Ht 7.

Applications:

The same as for Cv 19.

CV 21 (CONCEPTOR VESSEL POINT NO. 21)

Chinese name:

Xuanji (north star).

Location:

On the midline of the sternum, midway between Cv 22 and Cv 20, or midway between the articulations of the left and right rib with the sternum. Here, *xuan* means rotation, and *ji* means axis; xuanji is the name given to the second and third stars of the Big Dipper, opposite the zigong star. This point is above zigong point, so it is called xuanji.

Connections:

None.

Direction of strike:

Straight in and slightly upward into Cv 22.

Damage:

Local pain and qi drainage occur when Cv 21 is struck. However, it is not a point I would bother with; Cv 22 is just above it and is much more appropriate.

Set-up point:

None.

Antidote:

Same as for Cv 20.

Healing:

Innervation is by the anterior cutaneous branch of the first intercostal nerve. Irrigation is the same as for Cv 16.

Used for cough, asthma, pain in the chest, chronic bronchitis, spasm of the esophagus, and cardiac spasm.

Traditional indications include swollen pharynx, throat blockage, coughing, fullness and pain in the chest and ribs, and laryngomalacia (a condition characterized by paroxysmal attacks of breathing difficulty and stridor caused by flaccidity of the structure of the larynx in children).

Traditional functions are to send qi down and open the chest. To massage, press and hold the point, do fingertip percussion, and do rotations clockwise or counterclockwise for xu or shi conditions.

Use with Cv 22, Pc 6, Liv 3, Liv 14, Bl 17, Bl 18, Bl 19, St 36, Cv 12, St 25, Cv 4, St 40, and Sp 4 for esophageal spasm (plumb pit throat).

See Cv 20 for asthma.

Add to Cv 19 formula for pain in the chest.

Applications:

The same as for Cv 20.

CV 22 (CONCEPTOR VESSEL POINT NO. 22)

Chinese name:

Tiantu (heaven's prominence).

Location:

In the depression 0.5 cun above the suprasternal notch, between the left and right sternocleidomastoid muscles. In its deep position it is in the sternohyoid and sternothyroid muscles.

Connections:

Yin wei mai.

Direction of strike:

Straight in to the pit of the neck.

Damage:

This is one of the most deadly points in the body. It will cause immediate suffocation and brain death. Only an experienced acupuncturist is advised to needle this point, using a special method of tilting the head back. This is a window of the sky point. At the very least it will cause emotional trauma such as fear or grief. It will also affect the lungs greatly, causing coughing and gasping for air at least and death at most. This is one of the points that I teach students how to strike in women's self-defense classes and those workshops for law enforcement officers where only a short time is allocated (as usual) to their learning self-defense.

Set-up point:

Lu 5.

Antidote:

None. You could try CPR and stretching the anus sphincter, which has the effect of speeding up the breathing, if he is not breathing.

Healing:

Innervation is by the anterior branch of the supraclavicular nerve. Irrigation is by the arch of the jugular vein and the branch of the inferior thyroid artery. Deeper is the trachea and inferior is the posterior aspect of the sternum.

Used for cough, asthma, sudden hoarseness, sore throat, hiccups, bronchitis, pharyngitis, goiter, nervous vomiting, spasm of the esophagus, and disease of the vocal cords. Traditional indications include heavy wheezing, coughing blood and pus, hoarse voice, and early stages of tumor or nodular growth on the neck.

Tian means heaven, and *tu* means chimney; the location of this point corresponds to the upper end of the trachea, and it is like a chimney for the lungs. Its traditional functions are to promote the dispersing function of the lungs, resolve phlegm, stop cough, soothe asthma, clear the throat, regulate the qi circulation, subdue ascending qi, cool the throat, and clear the voice. It is also a point of communication with the yin wei mai (yin linking channel).

To massage, press in and down under the sternum and hold, or try vibration with the fingertip (not strong).

Use with dingchuan, Cv 17, St 40, Liv 3, Liv 14, Bl 20, Bl 43, Bl 17, Bl 13, Bl 23, Lu 1, Lu 5, Lu 7, Cv 18, Cv 19, Cv 20, and Kd 6 for bronchial asthma.

Use with Kd 27, Cv 17, Bl 13, Lu 1, Kd 7, Lu 8, Co 4, Lu 9, Liv 2, Liv 3, and St 40 for cough and wheezing induced by rheumatic heart disease.

Use with St 40, Liv 3, Co 4, Sp 4, Co 11, Lu 7, Gv 14, dingchuan, bailo, Gb 20, and Gb 21 for tumors or nodular growth on the neck.

Applications:

Any weapon struck to this area can cause death, although the finger jab or one-knuckle punch is probably the most dangerous. Slap the inside of his right elbow with your right palm at Lu 5; reloading the right elbow, bring it into Cv 22. You would want to be pretty sure that your life is threatened in using this method.

CV 23 (CONCEPTOR VESSEL POINT NO. 23)

Chinese name:

Lianquan (modesty's spring or screen spring).

Location:

Above the Adam's apple, in the depression at the upper border of the hyoid bone. In the depression between the pharyngeal prominence and the lower margin of the hyoid bone.

Connections:

Th/Pc and Bl/Kd divergent meridians and yin wei mai.

Direction of strike:

Upward at an angle of 45 degrees into the throat where it joins under the chin.

Damage:

This is a concentration point of shao yin (heart/kidney), although because of the location, you would not really worry about electrical damage sincethe physical damage to this area will cause death through suffocation anyway. It is possible to build up a whole heap of muscle in this area by performing the old wrestler's bridge often. This is what tricksters who perform the old chopstick-in-the-neck trick do. The chopstick is forced straight in where the heavy concentration of muscle is. However, we strike in an upward manner, thus getting past the muscle and into the trachea.

Set-up point:

None. Perhaps use neigwan as a qi drainage point, although this point needs no set-up point.

Antidote:

None.

Healing:

Innervation is by the branch of the cutaneous cervical nerve, the hypoglossal nerve, and the branch of the glossopharyngeal nerve. Irrigation is by the anterior jugular vein.

Used for swelling in the subglossal region, salivation with glossoplegia, aphasia with stiffness of the tongue, sudden hoarseness, difficulty swallowing, bronchitis, pharyngitis, tonsillitis, and paralysis of the hypoglossus muscle.

Traditional functions: a branch area of the spleen channel and a point of communication with the yin wei mai (yin linking channel). *Lian* here means clear, and *quan* means spring. In ancient times the two blood vessels below the tongue were called lianquan; this point is close to those vessels. It can treat stiffness of the tongue and ease throat.

To massage, press and hold, or do fingertip vibration.

Use with Si 17, Lu 11, Co 4, Co 11, Bl 10, Cv 22, Si 5, Si 3, Co 3, Th 1, St 36, St 40, Sp 6, Liv 2, Liv 3, Lu 5, and Lu 7 for tonsillitis and throat blockage.

Use with Gb 34, Liv 3, Pc 6, Ht 5, Cv 22, Gv 15, Co 4, Liv 1, Ht 7, Gv 26, Si 3, Kd 1, Sp 6, Gb 30, Kd 4, Gb 21, Th 21, and Th 17 for aphasia and paralysis of the hypoglossus muscle, stiffness of tongue, etc.

Applications:

You have to strike at a 45-degree angle. If you consider that the underside of the chin and that line where it joins with the neck make a 90-degree angle, then you must punch 45 degrees upward into that join. To do this, you do not have to actually angle your punch at 45 degrees; all you have to do is to use a method from the taijiquan small san-sau. He attacks with a right straight. You block with your left palm sliding downward onto neigwan as your right palm (facing upward) attacks to Ht 3 (fig. 313). All you now have to do is punch your right fist forward, aiming just under the chin at Cv 23; but as you do this, you flick your palm to palm down, and as you make the fist, the action causes your fist to flick upward and strike Cv 23 at the correct angle (fig. 314).

Figure 313

Figure 314

CV 24 (CONCEPTOR VESSEL POINT NO. 24)

Chinese name:
 Chengjiang (contains fluids or receives fluids).

Location:
 Cheng here means receiving, and *jiang* means fluid. The point is in the depression at the midpoint of the chin (in the center of the mentolabial groove, below the middle of the lower lip between the orbicularis oris and mentalis muscles) where excess saliva is received.

Connections:
 Colon and stomach.

Direction of strike:
 This point can be struck in a number of ways. Straight in, or from left to right or right to left.

Damage:
 Strike from the recipient's left to his right using either the tips of the fingers or the one-knuckle punch. This will cause extreme nausea, vomiting, and even a KO. Striking from the recipient's right to his left will also cause extreme nausea and vomiting, with great pain down the left side of the abdomen. This can be so great that he will buckle up in pain. When struck straight in it will knock his teeth out!

Set-up point:
 If striking left to right, you should slap down the inside of the attacker's right arm. If striking from right to left, you should slap up the outside of the attacker's forearm.

Antidote:
 Rub Cv 4 counterclockwise while maintaining mild pressure around the point for a strike that goes left to right. For the right-to-left strike, rub Cv 4 clockwise with mild pressure inward.

Healing:

Innervation is by a branch of the facial nerve. Irrigation is by the branches of the inferior labial artery and vein.

Used for facial paralysis, facial swelling, swelling of the gums, toothache, salivation, mental disorders, hemiplegia, and ulcers in the mouth.

Traditional indications include mouth and eyes awry, facial edema, emaciation and thirst, and hemiplegia.

Traditional functions are to dispel wind and stop pain. It is also a branch region of the colon channel.

Massage techniques include pressing and holding the point, doing rotations clockwise or counterclockwise for xu or shi conditions, doing fingertip percussion or vibration, and pressing in slowly with both thumbs and releasing quickly, pulling the thumbs apart.

Use with Co 19, Gb 20, Gb 21, St 44, St 45, St 5, St 6, St 7, St 8, St 4, St 2, St 36, St 40, Gb 34, Liv 3, and Liv 2 for facial paralysis and facial swelling or pain.

Use with Gv 16, Gv 15, Gv 14, Gb 20, Gb 21, Gb 41, Gb 34, Liv 3, Co 4, Gv 20, Si 3, Si 13, Si 14, Si 15, Th 15, Bl 12, Bl 13, Bl 17, and Bl 18 for headache and stiff neck.

Use with St 4, St 45, St 44, Liv 2, Co 4, Co 11, Co 1, and Co 2 for fever with blisters on the lips and mouth.

Applications:

Strike and slide down the inside of his left forearm to set up and block his right attack using your right palm. Then bring your right one-knuckle punch or fingertips back across his Cv 24 point from his left to his right.

Now you can seen that this meridian is the most dangerous. Most people know that the centerline points are dangerous, but few know why. In practice, stay away from these points. Pull your punches short of the points; even mild pressure to some of the more sensitive ones will cause damage and have long-term effects.

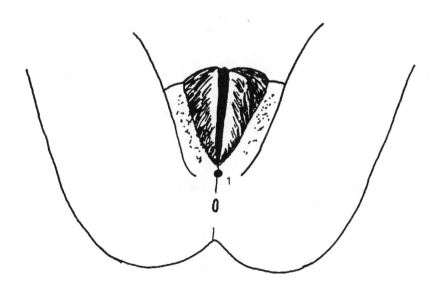

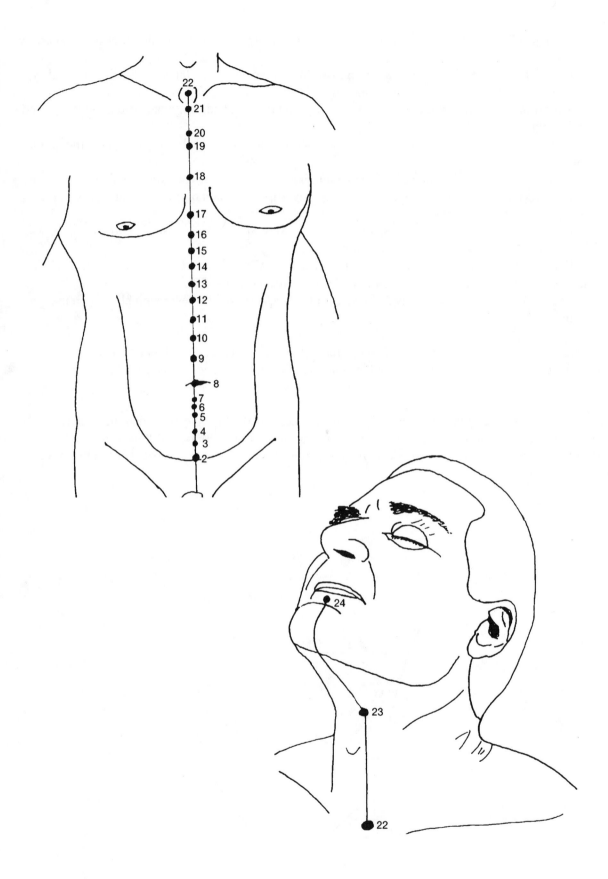

Chapter 2

The Governor Vessel (Du Mai)

The governor vessel, or du mai, begins in the area of the perineum and rises up the inside of the backbone to the nasal column. Again, the points on this meridian are very dangerous, as they run along the centerline of the body and especially over the center of the brain. Any of these points can cause death when struck hard, and some of the points, struck lightly, will cause considerable damage when the right weapon is used with the correct direction of the strike. The back points, of course, are harder to get at than those of the ren mai, but given the correct technique, it is not so difficult. In fact, many of the methods for getting to the bladder meridian will suffice when trying to get to Gv points. Most of these points do not need set-up points, although some are indicated. And most of them do not even need other strikes to additional points to enhance their danger.

The du mai is often referred to as "the sea of yang meridians" because the three yang meridians of both the feet and the hands converge into the du meridian at Gv 14. It regulates the circulation of qi and blood in the yang meridians, so it has the function of governing all the yang meridians.

The functions of the Cv meridian are to bind together all of the meridians in the body, regulate the circulation of blood and qi in the yang meridians, regulate the functional activities of the brain and the spinal marrow, and regulate the function of the urinary and reproductive systems.

Points on the Gv meridian are usually indicated for loss of consciousness, fever, infantile convulsion, malaria, urogenital disorders, malaria, psychosis, tension (rigidity) in the spinal column, neurasthenia, epilepsy, headache, impotence, leukorrhea, enuresis, diarrhea, and internal disorders due to a deficiency of yang qi. The purification points for qigong, where the qi is purified (distilled) into jing are also on the Gv meridian. (Jing is a form of purified qi; it can be equated as water is to steam—water can be heated and turned into steam to do work. So too is it with qi and jing.) The areas of the body physically associated with the Gv meridian are the brain, kidneys, marrow, uterus, eyes, nose, mouth, and lips.

When the Gv meridian is out of order, opisthotonos (a position of the body where the head, neck, and back are arched backward, as in tetanus) and syncope (fainting) can occur. A disorder along this meridian can also cause stiffness at the nape of the neck.

Coalescent points of the Gv meridian are Cv 1, Cv 24, and Si 3.

The partner to the Gv meridian is yang qiao mai. The Gv meridian is called the "husband"; the yang qiao mai is called the "wife."

GV 1 (GOVERNOR VESSEL POINT NO. 1)

Chinese name:

Changqiang (long strength).

Location:

Midway between the tip of the coccyx and the anus. *Chang* means long and *qiang* means strong; the spinal column is long and strong, and the point is located at the lower end of the spinal column below the tailbone.

Connections:

A crossing point of the kidney channel and a luo (connecting) point of the Gv channel. This collateral runs up beside the spine, crossing the spine and passing through all the jiaji points. It is connected to the gallbladder and kidney meridians.

Direction of strike:

Same as for Cv 1. Gv 1, however, is situated slightly back from Cv 1. Cv 1 is situated forward of the anus; Gv 1 is situated back toward the backbone from the anus.

Damage:

The damage here is great when struck straight up in to the point. It can cause unconsciousness, mental disorders, and also physical disorders to the anus. It is a luo point for the eight extra meridians, so qi damage here is great. It is the "sea of yang" point (the Cv 1 is called the "sea of yin," so a strike here will also unbalance the whole energy system of the body. It is not easy to get to though. I would consider other points before this one in a self-defense situation (not good sticking your toe up into his anus if you should miss!).

Set-up point:

You could use Gv 26 just under the nose. This will enhance the effect of causing unconsciousness and will cause KO all by itself or even death.

Antidote:

Gv 20, pressing downward. And you could massage Gv 1 if there is not too much physical damage here.

Healing:

Innervation is by the posterior ramus of the coccygeal nerve and the anal nerve. Irrigation is by the branches of the inferior hemorrhoid artery and vein, the vertebral venous plexus.

Used for hemafecia, diarrhea, constipation, hemorrhoids, prolapsed rectum, pain in the lower back, eczema of the scrotum, inducing labor, impotence, and psychosis.

Traditional indications include diarrhea, prolapsed anus, loss of sperm, cloudy and turbid urine, infantile convulsions, and madness.

Traditional functions are to regulate and clear obstructions from the Gv and Cv channels and promote the functions of the intestines. It can also have a lifting effect on the qi. It is a distal point for conditions affecting the brain.

To massage, press and hold the point or do rotations clockwise or counterclockwise for xu or shi conditions.

Use with Co 4, Sp 9, Sp 6, Gb 21, Bl 31, and Bl 32 for induction of labor.

Use with Bl 25, Bl 35, Bl 20, Gv 20, and Bl 57 for hemorrhoids and anal prolapse. You can also just apply pressure to this point for acute hemorrhoidal pain.

For spinal problems, use with Gv 14 and jiaji points from T1 to L5, Bl 23, Kd 3, Bl 40, Bl 60, and Si 3.

Applications:

Slap his left Th 8 point with your right palm as he attacks with a left strike. Bring your right reverse knife edge back to strike up under his nose at Gv 26 (fig. 315). You will now be able to get around behind him to attack to Gv 1 with your right knee (fig. 316).

Figure 315   **Figure 316**

GV 2 (GOVERNOR VESSEL POINT NO. 2)

Chinese name:
   Yaoshu (lower back's hollow).
Location:
   In the hiatus of the sacrum.
Connections:
   None.
Direction of strike:
   Upward into the sacrum.
Damage:
   This point does mainly physical damage to the lower backbone (mainly the sacrum) and the kidneys. It has to be struck quite hard to cause both physical damage and qi damage. So this is a point that I would not consider in a dire situation unless the attacker was standing still with his back to me. This point can do mental damage as well.
Set-up point:
   Same as for Gv 1.
Antidote:
   Massage Gv 1.
Healing:
   Innervation is by the branch of the coccygeal nerve. Irrigation is by the branches of the median sacral artery and vein.
   Used for irregular menstruation, pain and stiffness of the lower back, epilepsy, hemorrhoids, muscular atrophy, motor impairment/numbness and pain of the lower extremities, enuresis, and incontinence due to paraplegia.

47

Traditional functions: *yao* here means lower back, and *shu* means point; the point is in the lower back where the qi of the meridian is infused, and it can be used to strengthen the lower back.

To massage, press and hold the point; do rotations clockwise or counterclockwise for xu or shi conditions, press in slowly with both thumbs and release quickly, pulling the thumbs apart; do fingertip percussion or loose fist percussion; or do fingertip vibration.

Use with Bl 25, Bl 26, Bl 53, Bl 54, Bl 40, Gb 34, Gb 30, Gb 29, Bl 57, Bl 58, Bl 27, Bl 28, Bl 29, Bl 30, Bl 31, Bl 32, Bl 33, Bl 34, Bl 35, Gv 20, Si 3, Gb 39, and Bl 11 for lower back pain and stiffness.

Use with Gv 1, Gv 20, Bl 20, St 36, Sp 3, Bl 35, Bl 25, St 37, and Bl 57 for hemorrhoids.

Use with Bl 28, Bl 27, Bl 26, Bl 25, Bl 24, Bl 23, Bl 22, St 25, Cv 2, Cv 3, Cv 4, Cv 5, Cv 9, St 28, Bl 39, Sp 9, and Sp 6 for enuresis, incontinence, etc.

Applications:

Same as for Gv 1, only the strike, of course, is to Gv 2, upward and slightly in.

GV 3 (GOVERNOR VESSEL POINT NO. 3)

Chinese name:

Yaoyangguan (lumbar yang's hinge).

Location:

Yao here means lower back, yang is as in yin/yang, and guan here means gear. The Gv meridian is yang: this point pertains to it and is located in the turning region of the lower back, like the gear of the lumbar joint (also translated as loin's yang gate). Below the spinous process of the fourth lumbar vertebra, in the lumbodorsal fascia and the supraspinal and interspinal ligaments.

Connections:

None.

Direction of strike:

Straight in.

Damage:

You notice that people with weak kidneys have legs that are not too strong. When and if you begin to have kidney problems, the first symptom will be your legs becoming weaker. In particular, your knees will begin to buckle when, for instance, you climb higher stairs and you notice that whereas you could earlier bound up these stairs, now you have difficulty. This is because the kidneys control the knees; thus when the kidneys begin to go, so do the knees. This point controls kidney qi, and when struck, this control goes haywire, weakening the knees and the waist as well. So this point works really well with a strike to Sp 19, which also acts upon the opposite leg (of the strike).

A hard strike here, of course, will also damage the spinal disks in this area, so permanent physical damage could result.

Set-up point:

Sp 19.

Antidote:

Apply something warm to the kidney area, including the backbone and the point Gv 3. (This is in the case of a strike to Gv 3, and not to some pathogenic intrusion that is affecting the kidneys.)

Healing:

Innervation is by the medial branch of the posterior ramus of the lumbar nerve. Irrigation is by the posterior branches of the lumbar artery and vein and the vertebral venous plexus.

Used for pain in the lumbosacral region; muscular atrophy; motor impairment, numbness, and pain of the lower extremities; irregular menstruation; seminal emission; impotence; and chronic enteritis.

Traditional indications include irregular menstruation, vaginal discharge with blood, loss of sperm, diarrhea, lower abdominal distension, continuous vomiting, lower back pain, pain in the knees, numb and stiff lower limbs, and scrofula.

Traditional functions are to regulate the kidney qi, benefit the lower back and knees, and eliminate cold damp.

Massage techniques are the same as for Gv 2.

Use with Bl 23, Bl 24, Bl 25, Bl 26, Bl 52, Bl 53, Bl 54, Gv 4, Bl 40, Gb 34, and Gv 3 for lower back pain.

Use with Gv 4, Bl 23, Bl 24, Cv 4, Cv 6, Kid 3, Gb 25, St 36, Pc 6, and Liv 3 for impotence and seminal emissions.

Use with Bl 20, Bl 23, Bl 25, Bl 26, St 25, Cv 12, St 37, Sp 4, Sp 91, for diarrhea.

Applications:

As he attacks with a right straight, block with your right palm as your left comes underneath (as many times before in this book). Your right fingers are now clear to strike straight in to Sp 19. Swing him around using his right arm as a lever, putting his lower back within range for a knee strike to Gv 3.

GV 4 (GOVERNOR VESSEL POINT NO. 4)

Chinese name:

Mingmen (life's door, or gate of life).

Location:

Ming means life, and *men* means door. The kidneys are the source of life, and this point is between the shenshu (Bl 23 points that are like a door to the qi of the kidneys). Below the spinous process of the second lumbar vertebra, in the lumbodorsal fascia and the supraspinal and interspinal ligaments.

Connections:

None.

Direction of strike:

Straight in and slightly downward.

Damage:

This is the "gate of life" point, and great damage can be done with a hard strike downward to this point. The recipient will feel a "ring" of pain going around the waistline and rising upward into the head because this strike will affect the whole yang energy of the body and also will damage kidney jing, thus making him very sick. Left untreated, this strike could cause a delayed death point strike with the recipient dying up to two weeks later from qi stagnation and, finally, stoppage.

Set-up point:

Gb 25.

Antidote:

If the point has not been too badly damaged physically, you must have an acupuncturist treat it directly in the opposite direction, needling 3 fen upward.

Healing:

Innervation and irrigation are the same as for Gv 3.

Used for stiffness of the back, lumbago, leukorrhea, impotence, seminal emissions, diarrhea, lower back pain or strain, enuresis, endometritis, peritonitis, spinal myelitis, sciatica, nephritis, and sequelae of infantile paralysis.

Traditional indications include headache, tidal fever, infantile convulsions, pain in the lower back and abdomen, pain of intestinal colic, loss of sperm, vaginal discharge with blood, uterine bleeding, and prolapse of the anus.

Traditional functions are to promote and tonify kidney qi, tonify yang qi, control emissions, strengthen the lower back, and nourish the source qi (yuan qi).

Massage techniques are the same as for Gv 2.

Use with Gv 14, Bl 17, Co 1, St 36, Cv 12, Liv 3, Bl 20, and Sp 3 for iron deficiency anemia.

Use with Gv 20, Cv 4, Sp 6, Bl 33, Bl 23, Kd 3, Cv 2, Cv 3, and Cv 6 for enuresis.

See Gv 3 for treatment of impotence and spermatorrhea.

Use with Bl 23, Bl 20, Cv 4, Cv 6, Cv 12, Cv 9, St 28, St 36, Sp 9, and Sp 3 for copious urine in the elderly.

See Gv 3 for treatment of diarrhea.

Use with Bl 23, Kd 3, Th 4, St 36, C 12, Gb 25, Cv 4, Cv 6, and Sp 3, warming all with moxa for yang xu (deficient) conditions such as food in stool, watery diarrhea, etc.

Applications:

Slam his right straight with your left palm while your right palm attacks to Gb 25. You have stepped to your left. Move to the rear and strike straight in to Gv 4, using his shoulders as a lever backward, increasing the pressure of your knee at Gv 4. Drop the knee from slightly above the point, downward on the point.

GV 5 (GOVERNOR VESSEL POINT NO. 5)

Chinese name:

Xuanshu (suspended axis).

Location:

Below the spinous process of the first lumbar vertebra. *Xuan* here means suspended, and *shu* means pivot; the point is suspended as a pivot for lumbar movement when lying supine.

Connections:

None.

Direction of strike:

Slightly downward.

Damage:

Great physical pain with a spreading sensation around to the front of the body and up into the lungs. This strike causes one to breathe out deeply and to buckle up and fall down. It must, however, be struck right on the point using a smaller weapon such as a one-knuckle punch.

Set-up point:

Lu 5.

Antidote:

If no great physical damage has been done to the spine, then rest will usually heal this strike.

Healing:

Innervation and irrigation are the same as for Gv 3. Use for diarrhea with undigested food, pain and stiffness of the lower back, abdominal pain, dysentery, and prolapsed anus.

Traditional functions are to build yang qi, tonify yuan qi, and strengthen the lumbar region. Massage techniques are the same as for Gv 3.

Use with Gv 4, Gv 3, Gv 14, Gv 16, and Gv 20 for multiple neuritis.

Use with Bl 22, Bl 23, Gv 4, Bl 24, Bl 25, Bl 26, Bl 52, Bl 53, shiqizhuixia (an extra point below the fifth lumbar vertebra), Bl 40, Kd 3, Gb 34, and Gb 39 to strengthen the lumbar region.

Applications:

Strike his right attack at Lu 5 using the back of your right palm. Hook your palm over his right forearm and pull him around so that his back is now in view. This should be easy; the strike to Lu 5 drains qi and power greatly. Now strike to Gv 5 using a one-knuckle punch or a fist that turns right over so that the little finger side points upward. This is usually the type of fist to use when striking low on the body.

GV 6 (GOVERNOR VESSEL POINT NO. 6)

Chinese name:

Jizhong (middle of spine).

Location:

Ji here means spine, and *zhong* means middle. The spine has a total of 21 vertebrae; this point is below the spinous process of the 11th vertebra and is therefore in the middle of the spine.

Connections:

None.

Direction of strike:

Straight in and slightly downward.

Damage:

This point will cause much the same damage as for Gv 5. The only difference is that because of its location (same for the next two points), the effect is like being struck in the guts because the lungs will also be affected physically.

Set-up point:

Lu 5.

Antidote:

Same as for Gv 5.

Healing:

Innervation is by the medial branch of the posterior ramus of the 11th thoracic nerve. Irrigation is by the posterior branch of the 11th intercostal artery.

Used for jaundice, diarrhea, epilepsy, hepatitis, mid- to lower back pain, and paralysis of the lower limbs.

Massage techniques are the same as for Gv 3.

Use with Bl 18, Bl 19, Bl 20, Bl 25, Liv 14, Liv 3, Liv 2, Gb 24, Gv 9, Sp 9, jiaji points from T7 to T12, Liv 6, St 36, Sp 6, Gv 14, Liv 4, Liv 8, Gb 43, and Gb 44 for jaundice and/or hepatitis.

Use with Gv 11, Gv 2, Gv 1, Bl 11, Bl 17, Bl 18, Bl 20, Bl 27, Bl 28, Bl 23, Bl 40, Bl 57, Bl 58, Bl 62, Bl 63, Gb 34, Gb 39, Gv 16, and Gv 4 for back pain and stiffness.

See Gv 4 for diarrhea.

Applications:

Same as for Gv 5.

GV 7 (GOVERNOR VESSEL POINT NO. 7)

Chinese name:

Zhongshu (middle axis).

Location:

Zhong means middle and *shu* means pivot. This point is below the spinous process of the 10th thoracic vertebra and is like a pivot in the middle of the spine.

Connections:

None.

Direction of strike:

Straight in.

Damage:

Same as for Gv 6, only with even more lung damage with coughing and gasping for breath. This strike will also have an effect on the brain, with a rush of energy moving upward to shock the brain, and this can cause KO.

Set-up point:

Lu 5.

Antidote:

Put the patient's head between his legs and push lightly. This will stop the kick-in-the-guts feeling.

Healing:

Innervation is by the medial branch of the posterior ramus of the 10th thoracic nerve. Irrigation is by the posterior branch of the 10th intercostal artery.

Used for pain in the epigastric region, mid- to lower back pain and stiffness, stomach ache, cholecystitis, and diminishing vision.

Massage techniques are the same as for Gv 3.

Use with Gb 20, Gv 14, Bl 23, St 25, St 36, Bl 10, Gv 12, Gv 4, Bl 22, Co 4, Co 11, Gb 34, Cv 6, Cv 12, St 31, Liv 3, Lu 7, and Lu 1 for infantile paralysis.

Use with Bl 1, St 1, Gb 1, Liv 3, Co 4, Th 3, St 36, and Gv 20 for diminished vision.

Use with Bl 18, Bl 19, Bl 20, Liv 14, Gb 24, Liv 2, Gb 41, Gb 43, Gv 8, Gb 44, Liv 13, and Gv 9 for cholecystitis, jaundice, gall stones, etc.

Applications:

Same as for Gv 6.

GV 8 (GOVERNOR VESSEL POINT NO. 8)

Chinese name:

Jinsuo (sinew's shrinking).

Location:

Below the spinous process of the ninth thoracic vertebra.

Connections:

None.

Direction of strike:

Slightly downward and in.

Damage:

Again, this will have much the same effect as for Gv 7, only with more lung damage. Vision could also be lost temporarily should this strike be very hard. This strike can kill if done hard enough using, perhaps, an elbow.

Set-up point:

Slap the outside of the forearm at Co 10.

Antidote:

None. See a doctor immediately to repair the physical damage.

Healing:

Figure 317

Figure 318

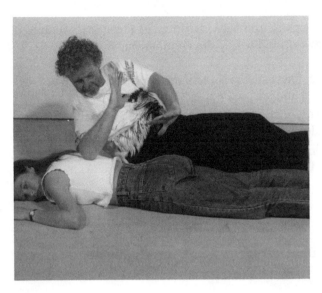

Figure 319

Innervation is by the medial branch of the posterior ramus of the ninth thoracic nerve. Irrigation is by the posterior branch of the ninth intercostal artery.

Used for epilepsy, stiffness and pain of the back, gastric pain, hepatitis, cholecystitis, pleurisy, hysteria, and intercostal neuralgia. Traditional functions: *jin* here means muscle or sinew, and *suo* means contracture. This point is useful for treating muscle contracture of all types.

Massage techniques are the same as for Gv 3.

Use with Gv 14, Si 3, Gb 34, Gv 12, Co 4, Liv 3, Gv 26, Kd 1, Bl 40, Bl 60, Bl 67, Bl 66, Gb 43, Gb 44, and St 36 for nonfebrile convulsions.

See Gv 7 for treatment of hepatitis, cholecystitis, etc.

Use with Pc 6, Pc 3, Pc 8, Ht 7, Kd 1, Gb 21, Gv 20, St 36, Liv 2, Liv 3, Liv 4, Liv 8, Co 4, Co 11, Cv 12, Bl 17, Bl 18, Bl 20, Bl 25, Bl 14, Bl 43, and Bl 15 for hysteria.

Applications:

Here you can use a nice grappling method. However, you must be proficient in grappling. He attacks with a straight right. Slam his Co 10 point with your left palm. As you step to your left, notice that your right arm is moving up over your left arm (fig. 317). Kick his forward lower leg with your right heel as both arms grab around his waist to lift him (fig. 318). Take him into the air, throwing him down face first and following him down with right elbow to Gv 8 (fig. 319). This method, of course, can be used anywhere on the backbone.

GV 9 (GOVERNOR VESSEL POINT NO. 9)

Chinese name:

Zhiyang (reaching yang).

Location:

Below the spinous process of the seventh thoracic vertebra, in the supraspinal and interspinal ligaments. Zhi here means reaching and yang is the yang of yin/yang. This point is at the level of the diaphragm, and the qi of this channel passes here on its ascension. It reaches the yang within yang above the diaphragm from the yin within yang below the diaphragm.

Connections:

None.

Direction of strike:

Straight in and slightly downward.

Damage:

This point too will affect the lungs, causing coughing and qi drainage. It will also have an effect upon the liver and gallbladder. The qi flow will be disrupted, and there will be physical damage to the spine as well. If struck hard enough, the fight will be over.

Set-up point:

Lu 5, Co 10, or St 3.

Antidote:

For spinal damage, see a doctor. For liver and gallbladder qi damage, see a TCM doctor.

Healing:

Innervation is by the medial branch of the posterior ramus of the seventh thoracic nerve. Irrigation is by the posterior branch of the seventh intercostal artery.

Used for cough, asthma, jaundice, pain in the chest and back, stiffness of the spinal column, hepatitis, cholecystitis, malaria, pleurisy, roundworm in the bile duct, stomachache, and intercostal neuralgia.

Traditional indications include cough, panting, chest and back pain, jaundice, a curled up and lethargic body, fullness in the chest, cold stomach, and intestinal noises.

This point's traditional function is to regulate the qi function, transform damp heat, expand the chest and diaphragm, and soothe the liver and gallbladder.

Massage techniques are the same as for Gv 3.

Use with Bl 17, Bl 18, Bl 12, Bl 13, Bl 43, Lu 1, Lu 7, Lu 5, Lu 8, Cv 7, Co 4, St 36, and Liv 3 for cough, asthma, colds, or flu-type symptoms.

See Gv 6 for treatment of hepatitis, jaundice, gall stones, cholecystitis, etc.

Use with Bl 17, Bl 18, Bl 19, Bl 20, Bl 16, Bl 15, Bl 43, Cv 17, Liv 14, Liv 13, Liv 3, and Pc 6 for fullness and pain in the chest.

Use with Bl 17, Bl 18, Bl 20, Bl 21, Bl 22, Bl 23, Bl 25, Cv 12, Cv 14, Cv 9, Cv 6, Cv 4, St 21, St 25, St 36, Kd 3, Sp 3, Sp 9, Liv 3, and Sp 6 for intestinal noises, lethargy, cold stomach, nausea, etc.

Applications:

Same as for Gv 8.

GV 10 (GOVERNOR VESSEL POINT NO. 10)

Chinese name:

Lingtai (spirit's platform).

Location:

Below the spinous process of the sixth thoracic vertebra, in the supraspinal and interspinal ligaments.

Connections:

None.

Direction of strike:

Slightly downward.

Damage:

This point strike will cause a loss of power by attacking the diaphragm (although not as much as a strike to Cv 17). There is obvious physical damage to the spine and central nervous system, and the heart may stop when a hard strike is felt. This point also has a damaging effect on the communication between spirit and mind, thus causing a detached feeling that gets worse if left untreated.

Set-up point:

Lu 5 or Lu 8 and Ht 5 together. You could also attack to Cv 17 as a set-up point, although the fight will be over as soon as it is attacked.

Antidote:

For a hard strike, most of these back Gv points require medical treatment and/or CPR because you are attacking the spine.

Healing:

Innervation is by the medial branch of the posterior ramus of the sixth thoracic nerve. Irrigation is by the posterior branch of the sixth intercostal artery and the venous plexus of the vertebra.

Used for cough, asthma, back pain, neck rigidity, furuncles, bronchitis, roundworm in the bile duct, malaria, and stomachache.

Traditional indications include hot or cold external attack (common cold), stiffness of the neck and soreness along the spine, prolonged cough and/or asthma, hot conditions in the spleen, boils, and carbuncles.

Traditional functions: *ling* here means spirit, and *tai* means platform. This point is below shendao (Gv 11) and xinshu (Bl 15) and is likened to a platform for the heart spirit. It regulates the qi in the channels, expels wind, cools heat, and resolves damp/phlegm.

Massage techniques are the same as for Gv 3.

Use with Gb 34, Pc 6, St 36, Gb 24, St 25, Cv 12, Bl 19, Cv 4, *dannangxue* (an extra point), and jiaji points from T8 to T9 for roundworm in the common bile duct.

Use with Gv 14, Gv 13, Pc 6, Pc 5, Co 11, Sp 10, Kid 7, Gb 34, Co 4, Lu 7, Lu 8, Si 3, Gv 12, Gv 16, Kid 3, Liv 3, Bl 11, St 31, Ht 7, Bl 20, Gb 39, Gv 4, and jiaji points from T3 to T12 for malaria.

Applications:

Strike his right wrist with your left knife-edge palm and grab violently, pulling downward onto Ht 5 and Lu 8. Your right palm will now strike downward onto Cv 17. Pull his right arm around so that his back is now in view for a strike using the right heel palm to Gv 10.

GV 11 (GOVERNOR VESSEL POINT NO. 11)

Chinese name:

Shendao (spirit's path).

Location:

Below the spinous process of the fifth thoracic vertebra.

Connections:

None.

Direction of strike:

Straight in.

Damage:

Obvious physical damage to the spine. This point also causes mental disorders—too much worry and grief, depression, and loss of memory—which will get worse as time passes. Palpitations will also be a part of one's life when this point is struck and not treated.

Set-up point:

Neigwan.

Antidote:

It is obviously difficult to treat this same point if physical damage is done. However, this is one of the only ways to treat the qi disorders caused by this strike, so see an acupuncturist.

Healing:

Innervation is by the medial branch of the posterior ramus of the fifth thoracic nerve. Irrigation is by the posterior branch of the fifth intercostal artery and the vertebral venous plexus.

Use for poor memory, anxiety, palpitations, cardiac pain, pain and stiffness of the back, cough, fever, heart disease, malaria, seizures, and intercostal neuralgia.

Shen means spirit or consciousness, and *dao* means path; the heart houses the shen, and the point is medial to xinshu (Bl 15), the shu point of the heart. Its traditional functions are to tonify heart qi, calm the shen, and regulate the qi flow. Massage techniques are the same as for Gv 3.

Use with Bl 14, Bl 15, Bl 43, Bl 17, Bl 18, Ht 7, Pc 6, Liv 3, Pc 7, and Pc 3 for palpitations, anxiety, heart disease, etc.

Use with Bl 12, Bl 13, Bl 43, Bl 17, Bl 18, Bl 20, Lu 7, Lu 5, Co 4, Lu 8, Bl 10, Gv 14, Bl 18, Bl 20, St 40, taiyang (an extra point), and Gb 8 for conjunctivitis. (Be careful not to cross-infect the eyes if there is only one infected.)

Applications:

Any of the previous strikes to the back points, such as the points on the bladder meridian.

See page 127 for GV 12 (Governor Vessel Point No. 12).

GV 13 (GOVERNOR VESSEL POINT NO. 13)

Chinese name:
Taodao (way of happiness).
Location:
Below the spinous process of the first thoracic vertebra, in the supraspinal and interspinal ligaments.
Connections:
Reunion of the internal branch from Bl 12.
Direction of strike:
Straight in.
Damage:
This point has the potential to cause the bones of the body to weaken over some time. It will also cause mental disorders and obvious spinal damage.
Set-up point:
A strike straight in to the upper tantien or "third eye" point in between the eyebrows will enhance the effects of this strike.
Antidote:
Same as for Gv 12.
Healing:
Innervation is by the medial branch of the posterior ramus of the first thoracic nerve. Irrigation is by the posterior branch of the first intercostal artery and the vertebral venous plexus.

Use for stiffness of the back, headache, malaria, febrile disease, seizures, psychosis, pulmonary tuberculosis, and spasms of the head, neck, and muscles.

Traditional indications include fever and chills, absence of sweating, tidal fever, headache, heaviness in the head and dizziness, infantile convulsions, consumptive disorders, hot sensations in the bones (associated with yin xu conditions), and stiffness along the spine.

This is a point of intersection with the bladder channel. Its traditional functions are to relieve exterior conditions, cool heat, calm the shen, and clear the mind. *Tao* here means to enjoy or to be happy, and *dao* means path. Qi of the zhang fu is gathered at the Gv meridian and ascends along this pathway.

Massage techniques are the same as for Gv 3.
Use with Bl 13, Co 4, Co 11, Bl 12, Gv 14, Lu 7, Lu 11, Co 1, Th 1, Liv 2, Liv 3, and St 36 for fever.
Use with Gv 26, Pc 6, St 40, Gv 14, Bl 17, Bl 18, Bl 19, Bl 20, Bl 25, Liv 3, Co 4, Co 11, Th 7, Gb 20, Bl 10, and Th 16 for seizures.

Use with Pc 5, Pc 6, Co 11, Co 4, Si 3, Th 2, Gv 14, Gb 34, and Sp 9 for malaria.

Use with Gb 20, Bl 10, Gb 21, Th 15, Si 3, Si 13, Si 14, Si 14, Bl 13, Bl 43, Bl 17, Bl 60, and Gb 34 for neck and back stiffness.
Applications:
Same as Gv 12.

GV 14 (GOVERNOR VESSEL POINT NO. 14)

Chinese name:
Dazhui (big vertebra).
Location:
Between the spinous process of the seventh cervical and the first thoracic vertebra, in the supraspinal ligament. *Da* means large, and *zhui* means vertebra; this point is below the prominence of the seventh cervical vertebra, which is the largest of the vertebra.
Connections:
Connects all of the yang meridians.

Direction of strike:

Either upward or downward, depending upon the effect you wish to create.

Damage:

With a downward strike, the recipient feels a great drainage of qi, causing him to want to sleep. A gross lack of energy is apparent, and even the raising of an arm is difficult. There is also obvious spinal damage. When the point is struck upward, it sends a rush of energy to the upper body, causing confusion and tearing of muscles when they are used, as in the case where he tries to strike you, etc. Both directions cause profuse sweating and weakness. This point is used when a strike has caused a detachment between heaven and earth and the patient has a detached feeling, scattered mind, etc. This point can be tapped lightly with the fingers to revive someone who is perhaps tired while driving a car. Or you can place some ice over the point to cause sleep.

Set-up point:

Drain power by first slapping downward on Cv 17.

Antidote:

The same point is used, either tapping as in the case of a downward strike or gently rubbing downward in the case of an upward strike.

Healing:

Innervation is by the posterior ramus of the eighth cervical nerve and the medial branch of the posterior ramus of the first thoracic nerve. Irrigation is by the branch of the transverse cervical artery and the vertebral venous plexus.

Used for febrile disease, malaria, common cold, afternoon fever, cough, asthma, neck rigidity, stiffness of the back, epilepsy, heat stroke, psychosis, bronchitis, pulmonary tuberculosis, emphysema, hepatitis, blood disease, eczema, hemiplegia, and pain in the back of the shoulder.

Traditional indications include cold-induced disease, fever and chills, tidal fever, cough, constricted feeling in the chest and soreness in the ribs, and hot sensations in the bones with recurrent fever (xu yin associated), seizures, and congested throat.

As a point of intersection with the yang channels (Co, Si, Th, Bl, Gb, St), this point's traditional functions are to regulate the yang channels, relieve exterior conditions, eliminate wind cold, clear the mind, calm the shen, and clear heat.

Massage techniques are the same as for Gv 3.

Use with Bl 10, Gb 20, Gb 21, Th 15, Si 15, Si 14, Si 13, Si 12, Si 10, Si 9, Si 3, Bl 11, Bl 12, Bl 13, Bl 14, Bl 15, Bl 16, Bl 17, Bl 18, dingchuan, bailao, Gb 34, and Bl 60 for stiffness and pain of the neck, shoulders, and upper back.

Use with Bl 10, Gb 20, Bl 12, Bl 13, Lu 7, Co 4, Co 11, and Lu 5 for influenza.

Use with Sp 6, Kid 3, Lu 9, Lu 1, Gv 2, Liv 13, and Pc 5 for tidal fever.

Use with dingchuan, Bl 12, Bl 13, Bl 43, Bl 17, Bl 20, Bl 23, Kid 7, St 40, St 36, Liv 3, Liv 13, Liv 14, Cv 17, Cv 22, Lu 1, Lu 5, Lu 7, Lu 9, and Co 4 for asthma.

Applications:

Use Cv 17 as the setup, slapping it downward; turn him around and strike into Gv 14.

GV 15 (GOVERNOR VESSEL POINT NO. 15)

Chinese name:

Yamen (door of muteness).

Location:

At the midpoint of the nape, 0.5 cun above the natural hairline, in the depression 0.5 cun below Gv 16.

Connections:

Yang wei mai.

Direction of strike:

Struck straight in and slightly upward.

Damage:

Now we come to some of the most dangerous point strikes. Gv 15 will cause KO at the very least and death at the most. You can also strike to other dangerous points, such as Bl 10 and Gb 20 at the same time, but why bother? This point all by itself will cause enough damage to send you to jail for using excessive force! In between KO and death, we have such strange effects as the recipient's becoming mute, experiencing extreme dizziness, and even developing deafness and schizophrenia. It would be overkill to use this point.

Set-up point:

Neigwan.

Antidote:

The same point is treated using needles or finger pressure. Caution is advised here so as not to puncture the medulla oblongata.

Healing:

Innervation is by the third occipital nerve. Irrigation is by the branches of the occipital artery and vein.

Used for mental disorders, epilepsy, sudden hoarseness, stiffness of the tongue and post-apoplexy aphasia, headache, deaf-mutism, cerebral palsy, incomplete maturation of the brain, hysteria, and convulsions.

Traditional indications include occipital headache, stiff neck, nosebleed, stiff tongue inhibiting speech, apoplexy, insanity, and convulsions.

Traditional functions: *ya* here means mutism, and *men* means door; this is a point of intersection with the yang wei mai channel, which gives it the ability either cause or treat mutism, so it is likened to a two-way door. It removes obstructions from channels and collaterals, relieves hoarse voice, treats deaf-mutism, and clears the senses and consciousness.

Massage techniques include pressing and holding the point, doing rotations clockwise or counterclockwise for xu or shi conditions, pressing in with both thumbs and pulling laterally, and doing fingertip percussion.

Use with Gv 26, Si 3, St 40, Bl 20, Bl 18, Bl 19, Bl 17, Bl 15, Bl 14, Bl 13, Bl 43, Bl 22, Bl 25, Bl 23, Bl 24, Bl 26, Bl 66, Liv 3, Gv 14, Gv 16, Gb 20, Bl 62, Co 4, Pc 6, Pc 5, and Cv 12.

Use with Ht 5, Ht 7, Sp 6, Gb 34, and Liv 14 for seizures.

Use with Gv 16, Bl 10, Gb 20, Gb 21, Th 15, Si 3, Si 13, Si 14, Si 15, Bl 11, Bl 12, Bl 13, Bl 17, Bl 18, Bl 43, Bl 60, and Gb 34 for stiff neck, occipital headache.

Use with Th 6, Bl 66, Th 8, Th 1, Gv 20, Kd 1, and Liv 3 for mutism.

Applications:

You might be in a grappling situation. Your palm can easily reach around behind the top of the neck on the backbone and strike straight in, slightly upward. Or the point can be accessed when you are grappling and the opponent has his back toward you.

GV 16 (GOVERNOR POINT NO. 16)

Chinese name:

Fengfu (wind's dwelling).

Location:

Directly below the external occipital protuberance, in the depression between the trapezium muscles of both sides, 1 cun within the natural hairline at the back of the head.

Connections:

Yang wei mai.

Direction of strike:

Straight in.

Damage:

If there is a more dangerous point than Gv 15, then this is it. Its location is over important "life centers" of the body, such as the respiratory center located in the rhombic depression of the fourth venticula. Again, a strike here will cause KO in the very least and death at the most, with things like dizziness and mental disorders in between. A long-term effect of this strike is that the sensory organs will slowly lose their potency, with the sense of smell being the first to go. This point has a direct connection to the "sea of marrow," or the brain, so any strike here is devastating. This strike should not be used in the case where you just wish to control the attacker. It must be a very serious situation to use this point.

Set-up point:
Si 5, to increase the mental disorders and knockout.

Antidote:
Use Gv 16 with Si 5 and/or Si 3 and Gv 20, massaging each point in turn or using very careful needling methods.

Healing:
Innervation is by the branches of the third occipital nerve and the great occipital nerve. Irrigation is by the occipital artery.

Used for headache, neck rigidity, blurring of vision, epistaxis, sore throat, post-apoplexy aphasia, mental disorders, hemiplegia, numbness of the limbs, common cold, and stroke.

Traditional functions: this is a point of intersection with the yang wei mai and the yang qiao mai channels, and the latter channel enters the brain at this point. *Feng* means pathogenic wind, and *fu* here means place or dwelling. This is a point for eliminating pathogenic wind, and it also relieves headache and clears the mind.

Massage techniques are the same as for Gv 15.

Use with Gv 14, Gv 20, Co 11, Gb 20, Gb 21, Bl 10, Th 15, Si 3, Si 13, Si 14, Si 15, Bl 60, Bl 17, Bl 18, Bl 11, Bl 12, Bl 13, Bl 14, Bl 15, Bl 16, and Gb 34 for stiff neck, occipital headache, and upper back, shoulder, and neck pain and restriction.

Use with Gv 26, Lu 11, Sp 1, Pc 7, Bl 62, St 6, Cv 24, Pc 8, Gv 23, Cv 1, Co 11, Gv 20, Gv 14, Pc 6, Ht 5, Ht 7, Ht 8, Kd 1, St 40, Bl 20, Bl 18, Liv 3, Kd 4, Co 4, Si 19, and Pc 5 for mental disorders.

Applications:
The same as for Gv 15.

GV 17 (GOVERNOR VESSEL POINT NO. 17)

Chinese name:
Naohu (brain's household).

Location:
1.5 cun above Gv 16, superior to the margin of the occipital protuberance.

Connections:
Bladder.

Direction of strike:
In and slightly upward.

Damage:
This is an extremely dangerous point. It is situated close to foramen magnum, said to be the "gate of the brain." It will cause KO at least and death at the most. There will be dizziness to the extreme with falling down, and aphonia in between the two extremes.

Set-up point:
A slice down the outside of the forearm will set up this point.

Antidote:
Gb 20 points squeezed upward.

Healing:
Innervation is by the branch of the great occipital nerve. Irrigation is by the branches of the occipital arteries and veins of both sides.

Used for epilepsy, dizziness, pain and stiffness of the neck, insomnia, and headache.

This is a point of intersection with the bladder channel. *Nao* means brain, and *hu* means door. The Gv meridian runs upward along the spine and enters the brain at Gv 16. This point is like a door on the occipital protuberance for the qi of the meridian to the brain.

Massage techniques are the same as for Gv 3.

Use with Gv 16, Gb 20, taiyang, the extra point yintang, Bl 10, Gb 21, Co 4, Co 11, Liv 3, St 36, Gb 14, Gv 20, and Gv 14 for headache.

Use with formula listed under Gv 16 for neck and shoulder pain and stiffness.

Use with Gv 20, Gb 20, Pc 6, Ht 7, St 36, Liv 3, Cv 17, Gb 21, and Kd 1 for insomnia.

Applications:

He attacks with a left straight. Your right palm slices down the outside of his forearm as you step to your right. Your left palm also immediately slices down the forearm, thus turning him so that the back of his head is in view. Your right palm now slaps upward into the point.

GV 18 (GOVERNOR VESSEL POINT NO. 18)

Chinese name:

Qiangjian (between strength).

Location:

1.5 cun above Gv 17, midway between Gv 16 and Gv 20.

Connections:

None.

Direction of strike:

Straight in to the back of the head.

Damage:

A straight in strike will send a shock wave into the brain, thus causing KO. This is quite a well-known KO point, and many have demonstrated its ability to cause KO with relatively little pressure.

Especially if used with the set-up strike, this point causes the recipient to fall down and have a heavy feeling in his head. It requires much work for him to stand up again.

Set-up point:

Same as for Gv 17—slice down the outside of the forearm.

Antidote:

Pinch both Gb 20 points upward using the thumb and forefinger points.

Healing:

Innervation and irrigation are the same as for Gv 17.

Use for mania, headache, blurring of vision, neck rigidity, insomnia, and seizures.

Qiang here means stiffness and *jian* here means middle; this point is between the parietal and occipital bones, and its traditional functions are to treat stiff neck and headache.

Massage techniques are the same as for Gv 3.

Use with Gv 16, Gv 14, dingchuan, bailao, Gb 20, Bl 10, Gb 21, Th 15, Si 13, Si 14, Si 15, Si 3, Co 4, Gb 34, Bl 12, Bl 13, Bl 14, Bl 15, Bl 16, Bl 17, Bl 18, Bl 60, and Co 18 for stiff neck.

Use with Bl 1, Gb 1, Th 23, St 1, Gb 14, Liv 3, Gv 20, Gb 20, and Co 4 for blurred vision.

Applications:

Same as for Gv 17, only strike straight in to Gv 18.

GV 19 (GOVERNOR VESSEL POINT NO. 19)

Chinese name:

Houding (behind top).

Location:

Hou means posterior, and *ding* here means vertex; the point is posterior to the vertex, 1.5 cun above Gv 18 and 1.5 cun behind Gv 20, on the midline.

Connections:

None.

Direction of strike:

Straight down into the top of the back of the skull, going in at an angle of 45 degrees.

Damage:

Even a light blow right on target will cause shock to the brain as well as great local pain caused by an energy drainage. The pain here is so great that a light to medium blow will force the recipient to sit down. The point is fairly well protected here by the skull, but it is the shock wave that does the damage.

Set-up point:

Same as for Gv 18.

Antidote:

Gb 20.

Healing:

Innervation and irrigation are the same as for Gv 17.

Used for mania, epilepsy, headache, vertigo, migraine, common cold, and insomnia.

Because of its position posterior to the vertex, this point treats vertex pain and pain in the neck. Massage techniques are the same as for Gv 3.

Use with Gv 24, Gv 23, Gv 22, Gv 21, Gv 20, Gb 20, Gb 19, Si 5, Sp 2, Sp 4, Bl 67, Bl 63, Bl 62, St 40, St 36, Cv 12, Bl 20, Th 17, Gb 21, Bl 17, and Bl 18 for vertigo.

Use with Bl 1, Gb 1, Th 23, St 1, Liv 3, Liv 14, Bl 23, Lu 6, Bl 2, Bl 60, Gb 20, Co 4, and Sp 6 for blindness.

Applications:

Same as for Gv 18.

GV 20 (GOVERNOR VESSEL POINT NO. 20)

Chinese name:

Baihui (hundred meetings).

Location:

7 cun above the posterior hairline, at the intersection of the median line at the vertex, with a line drawn from the from the angle of the jaw through the apex of the ear and over to the apex of the other ear, in the galea aponeurotica, to the left and right of which are commonly found parietal foramen.

Connections:

Liv, Bl, and Th divergent meridians.

Direction of strike:

Straight down onto the top of the head, slightly back from the tip of the ear where it makes a line upward over the skull.

Damage:

Bahui is one of the points that are used for many healing applications. It is also a knockout point where a medium to hard strike is concerned. The point has to be struck right on using the heel palm, or else you should use the whole palm in a slapping type motion to also get the "inner square" group of extra points (covered in the chapter on the extra points). It is difficult to get to, however, unless you have the techniques to get at it. Local pain from qi drainage weakens the legs. This strike will also cause the attacker to go into shock.

Set-up point:

Si 17.

Antidote:

First press Gb 20 points, then press Co 10 hard, causing a twitch from the patient. If he doesn't twitch, then use CPR because he is dead! Press up into Gv 26 for the shock.

Healing:

Innervation is by he branch of the great occipital nerve and the frontal nerves. Irrigation is by the plexus at the anastomosis of the left and right superficial temporal artery and vein, in the deep position, by the emissary vein.

Used for mental disorders, apoplexy, headache, dizziness, tinnitus, blurring of vision, nasal obstruction, prolapse of rectum, shock, hypertension, insomnia, and seizures.

Traditional indications include headache, pain at the vertex, dizziness, tinnitus, deafness, nasal congestion, stroke, locked jaw, hemiplegia, madness, prolapsed anus, prolapsed uterus, and hemorrhoids.

Bai here means hundred, and *hui* means meeting; this point is at the vertex and is the meeting place for the 3-foot yang meridians (Gb, Bl, St) and the liver channel. Its traditional functions are to clear the senses and calm the spirit, ease the liver, eliminate wind, recapture yang, promote resuscitation, and strengthen the ascending function of the spleen.

To massage, press and hold the point; do rotations clockwise or counterclockwise for xu or shi conditions; press in slowly with both thumbs and release quickly, pulling the thumbs apart; and do fingertip percussion. You can do an energy transference from this point to tantien by placing the left laogong point (Pc 8) over Gv 20 and the right laogong point over the tantien region. This can take excess qi from the head and return it to the source (tantien).

Use with Gv 26, Pc 6, Liv 3, and Cv 12 for shock.

Use with the extra point yintang, taiyang, Gb 20, Co 4, Liv 2, Liv 3, Bl 18, Bl 19, Gb 21, Gb 34, Liv 4, and Liv 8 for headache at the vertex.

Use with Gv 1, Bl 35, Bl 57, Bl 25, Cv 12, St 36, Bl 37, St 25, Liv 3, and Th 4 for prolapsed anus.

Use with Cv 4, Cv 6, abdomen zigong (an extra point), St 36, Sp 6, Cv 12, Sp 3, Bl 20, and Bl 18 for prolapsed uterus.

Use with Ht 7, Pc 6, Kd 3, Kd 1, Gb 21, Pc 7, yintang, anmien (an extra point), and Sp 6 for insomnia.

Applications:

Strike the inside of his right elbow at Lu 5 with your right knife edge as your left knife edge strikes to Pc 7. Your left palm controls his right wrist as your right knife edge attacks to Si 17, just under the tip of the jaw angle. Wrap your right palm around his neck and pull his head forward, bending him at the waist. (You will be able to do this easily because of the strikes you have already executed.) Your right elbow is now able to strike straight in to Gv 20 with devastating results.

GV 21 (GOVERNOR VESSEL POINT NO. 21)

Chinese name:

Qianding (before top).

Location:

Qian here means front, and *ding* means vertex; the point is in front of the vertex, 1.5 cun anterior to Gv 20.

Connections:

None.

Direction of strike:

Straight down onto the crown, that little sunken bit on top of the head.

Damage:

Shock to the brain causing knockout. Power leaves the body, and then the legs go weak and there is nausea. This strike can cause brain dysfunction and death if the correct weapon is used.

Set-up point:

Same as for Gv 20.

Antidote:

Place hands over Gv 20 and hold lightly until the qi has risen again. Or squeeze Co 10 hard.

Healing:

Innervation on the communicating site of the branch of the frontal nerve with the branch of the great occipital nerve. Irrigation is by the anastomotic network formed by the right and left superficial temporal arteries and veins.

Used for epilepsy, dizziness, blurring of vision, headaches at the vertex, rhinorrhea, rhinopolypus, and infantile convulsions.

Massage techniques are the same as for Gv 20.

Use with Gv 26, Gb 21, St 40, Gb 20, Kd 1, St 2, St 3, St 4, Kd 6, St 5, St 6, St 7, St 8, Liv 3, Si 18, Co 4, and Sp 6 for puffy face.

Use with Gv 23, Gv 20, Si 5, Co 4, Th 1, Bl 60, Gb 43, Gb 20, Gb 21, Gb 34, Gb 41, Co 11, and Liv 3 for headache caused by wind.

Use with Gb 20, Co 4, Co 20, the extra point *bitong*, yintang, Bl 2, Gb 20, Lu 7, Gv 23, Bl 10, Bl 12, and Gv 14 for rhinorrhea.

Applications:

Same as for Gv 20.

GV 22 (GOVERNOR VESSEL POINT NO. 22)

Chinese name:

Xinhui (fontanelle's meeting).

Location:

Xin here refers to the fontanelle, and *hui* here means closing. The point is 3 cun anterior to Gv 20, 2 cun posterior to the anterior hairline.

Connections:

None.

Direction of strike:

Straight down onto the head, farther to the front.

Damage:

Blurred vision or temporary blindness. A shock wave travels down to the front of the chest, causing disorientation. Pain will happen a few minutes after the strike.

Set-up point:

Neigwan.

Antidote:

Apply pressure downward onto the point or needle it 5 cun horizontal along the skin to the rear.

Healing:

Innervation is by the branch of the frontal nerve. Irrigation is by the anastomotic network formed by the superficial temporal artery and vein and the frontal artery and vein.

Used for headache, blurring of vision, rhinorrhea, vertigo, rhinopolypus, and infantile convulsions.

Traditional functions are to treat headache and blurring vision.

Massage techniques are the same as for Gv 20.

Use with Gv 20, Gv 21, Gv 23, Gv 24, Gv 25, Gv 27, bitong, Bl 2, Gb 20, Co 4, Co 20, Co 11, St 2, St 3, yintang, St 40, Lu 5, and Lu 7 for rhinopolypus.

Use with Gb 3, Gb 4, Gb 20, St 7, St 2, St 40, Gv 20, Th 17, Th 21, Th 1, Th 3, Th 2, Si 16, Co 5, Co 4, Liv 2, Liv 3, and Kd 3 for tinnitus and deafness.

Applications:

Strike his right neigwan with your left knife edge to his right hook as your right palm slams downward into Gv 22.

GV 23 (GOVERNOR VESSEL POINT NO. 23)

Chinese name:

Shangxing (upper star).

Location:

1 cun within the anterior hairline, 4 cun anterior to Gv 20, on the midline. At the border between the left and right frontalis muscles.

Connections:

None.

Direction of strike:

Straight down into the front of the head.

Damage:

This strike will cause momentary blindness or blurred vision, as well as nasal problems in the long term. Qi drainage will also cause local pain.

Set-up point:

Neigwan.

Antidote:

Treat the same point with massage.

Healing:

Innervation is by the branch of the frontal nerve. Irrigation is by the branches of the frontal artery and vein and the branches of the superficial temporal artery and vein.

Used for headache, ophthalmoplegia, rhinorrhea, epistaxis, mental disorders, rhinopolypus, keratitis, and sore eyes.

Traditional indications include severe headache, facial edema, extra tissue in the nose, nosebleeds, sinus, dizziness, sore eyes, myopia, febrile disease where there is no sweating, and seizures.

Shang here means upper, and *xing* here refers to star; the head is considered as heaven, and this point is like a star in the heaven. Its traditional functions are to eliminate wind heat and remove nasal obstruction.

Massage techniques are the same as for Gv 20.

Use with Gv 25, Co 4, Co 11, Co 20, Co 1, Co 2, St 44, St 45, Sp 10, and Gb 20 for nosebleed.

Use with Gv 20, Co 4, Gb 20, Liv 2, Liv 3, Co 11, Gb 21, yintang, and taiyang for headache.

See Gv 22, for treatment of nasal polyps.

Use with Co 4, Co 11, Co 20, bitong, Bl 2, Bl 7, Liv 3, taiyang, Gb 20, St 40, and Lu 7 for rhinnitis.

Applications:

Same as for Gv 22.

GV 24 (GOVERNOR VESSEL POINT NO. 24)

Chinese name:

Shenting (spirit's hall).

Location:

On the midsagittal line of the head, 0.5 cun within the anterior hairline.

Connections:

Bladder and stomach.

Direction of strike:

Straight in to the forehead, .5 cun within the hairline on the meridian.

Damage:

This point can cause brain damage if struck hard enough. Many people actually use head butts with this point, but they are looking for health troubles in doing so. Always use the side of your forehead when giving a head butt. It is difficult to get a KO because there is much protection here. Better to use Gb 14 or 15.

Set-up point:

Neigwan.

Antidote:

Use Ht 6, pressing one inch down from the wrist flexure over the point with medium pressure and penetration.

Healing:

Innervation is by the branch of the frontal nerve. Irrigation is by the branches of the frontal artery and vein.

Used for epilepsy, anxiety, palpitations, insomnia, headache, vertigo, rhinorrhea, rhinopolypus, and stomatis.

Shen means spirit or mind, and *ting* here means vestibule or hall. The brain is the mansion of the primordial mind, and mind/consciousness and shen all reside in the brain and are seen as one. The point is on the forehead, like a vestibule/hall of the brain, and it is a point of intersection with the bladder channel.

Massage techniques are the same as for Gv 20. Use with Gv 16, Gb 20, Gv 14, Gv 26, Gv 23, Gv 20, Bl 62, Kd 6, Pc 6, Pc 5, Ht 5, Co 4, Liv 3, Sp 6, Gb 34, Cv 14, Cv 12, St 40, taiyang, and Gb 20 for epilepsy.

Use with Bl 14, Bl 15, Bl 17, Bl 18, Bl 20, Bl 43, Cv 17, Cv 12, Cv 14, Pc 6, Co 4, Co 11, St 36, Liv 3, and Sp 6 for anxiety, palpitations, insomnia, etc.

Applications:

Slap his right neigwan, controlling your with your left hand. Your right palm now comes back with a slap into Gv 24.

(GV 25) GOVERNOR POINT NO. 25

Chinese name:

Suliao (plain seam).

Location:

Su here is referring to the nasal cartilage, and *liao* means foramen; the point is in the foramen at the lower end of the nasal cartilage (at the tip of the nose).

Connections:

None.

Direction of strike:

Straight in at the tip of the nose.

Damage:

A whack on the nose is not nice at any time. It causes yang qi drainage and shock. This is an obvious point to strike, causing physical damage as well as great local pain and nosebleed. In the healing area, this point can be used in lieu of Gb 20 as a shock point and for low blood pressure. It will have an effect upon the lungs, since the lungs are expressed in the nose. A whack here obviously causes the senses to be confused, and, by the same token, healing using this point will clear the senses.

Set-up point:

None really, although neigwan could be used.

Antidote:

Gb 20.

Healing:

Innervation is by the external nasal branch of the anterior ethmoid nerve. Irrigation is by the lateral nasal branches of the facial artery and vein.

Used for loss of consciousness, nasal obstructions, epistaxis, rosacea, shock, low blood pressure, bradycardia, brandy nose, nosebleed, and rhinitis.

Traditional indications include extra tissue in the nose, runny nose, and infantile convulsions.

Its traditional functions are to raise and recapture the yang, rescue the patient from collapse, restore consciousness, clean the senses, and drain heat.

To massage, pinch the tip of the nose, press the point with the tip of the thumb or forefinger and hold, or rotate clockwise or counterclockwise for xu or shi conditions.

Use with Co 20, Co 4, Co 11, Liv 2, Liv 3, Liv 14, Liv 4, Liv 8, Sp 10, Liv 13, and St 36 for brandy nose.

Use with Pc 6, Kd 1, Liv 3, and Gv 26 for electric shock.

Use with Pc 6, St 36, Co 4, and Liv 3 for septic shock.

Applications:

A whack on the nose is a whack on the nose!

GV 26 (GOVERNOR VESSEL POINT NO. 26)

Chinese name:

Renzhong (philtrum).

Location:

Below the nose, a little above the midpoint of the philtrum (approximately one-third of the distance from the bottom of the nose to the top of the lip). In the orbicularis oris muscle.

Connections:

Colon and stomach.

Direction of strike:

Straight up into where the nose meets the upper lip, just a tad down from the nose. In fact, it is one-third of the distance between the nose and upper lip, down from the nose.

Damage:

This is a classic revival point for shock. However, when struck it gives shock and upsets the qi balance of the whole body. This area is very sensitive, having a whole heap of nerves in this area. A hard strike here will cause death or KO at least, with the whole body going into spasm from the nerve strike. You can test this point by having someone stand, bent at the waist. Try and push his waist to upright with him resisting. It is very difficult. Now, place only one finger across the point and press upward; he will stand up immediately. Only a light tap here is enough to cause shock. It is one of the more dangerous points.

Set-up point:

Th 8 will work fine with this point.

Antidote:

Work on Gb 21 slap the points on both sides and wipe away violently. You could also use Gv 20 pressing downward and the fish's belly point midway between the eyebrows pressing in and slightly downward.

Healing:

Innervation is by the buccal branch of the facial nerve and the branch of the infraorbital nerve. Irrigation is by the superior labial artery and vein.

Used for mental disorders, epilepsy, infantile convulsions, coma, trismus, facial paralysis, swelling of the face, pain and stiffness of the lower back, shock, heat exhaustion, hysteria, psychosis, motion sickness, nose disease, and halitosis.

Traditional indications include apoplectic locked jaw, unconsciousness, convulsions, seizures and insanity, mouth and eyes awry, facial edema, lip tremor, emaciation and thirst even after drinking, jaundice, edema, and twisting pain in the region of the heart and abdomen.

This point was called *shuigou* in ancient times. *Shui* means water, and *gou* means groove; the point is in the philtrum, which looks like a water groove. Traditional functions are to clear the senses and cool heat, calm the shen, benefit the lumbar spine, promote resuscitation and restore consciousness, eliminate wind, and act as a sedative.

To massage, press and hold the point, do rotations clockwise or counterclockwise for xu or shi conditions, do vibration or fingertip percussion, press in slowly with both thumbs and release quickly, pulling the thumbs apart.

Use with Pc 6, Kd 1, St 36, Co 4, Liv 3, Gv 25, and Cv 17 for septic shock.

Use with Cv 1, Cv 17, Liv 3, Bl 12, Bl 13, Lu 1, Kd 7, and mouth-to-mouth resuscitation for revival from drowning.

Use with Bl 40, Bl 25, Bl 26, Bl 23, Bl 52, Bl 53, Bl 54, Gb 34, for lower back pain, strain, and stiffness.

Use with Co 4, Ht 7, Pc 6, Liv 2, Liv 3, Kd 1, Gb 21, and Gv 20 for hysteria.

Use with Si 3, St 40, Liv 3, Gb 34, Gv 16, Gb 20, Gv 14, Bl 62, Kd 6, Sp 6, Cv 12, Cv 14, Ht 7, Gv 24, Pc 5, and Pc 6 for seizures.

Use with Kd 1, Pc 8, Gb 20, Pc 6, Co 4, Cv 4, Cv 6, St 36, St 40, Liv 4, Liv 3, and Liv 8 for stroke.

Use with St 5, St 6, St 7, St 8, Liv 3, Gb 21, Gb 34, Co 4, St 36, St 44, and St 45 for lockjaw.

Traditional functions are as a point of intersection with the colon and stomach channels. (Ren also means man, and zhong also means middle, so this point name also translates as middle of man.)
Applications:

Strike his left forearm at Th 8, and rebound your right palm back to under his nose at Gv 26, using the index finger side of your palm.

GV 27 (GOVERNOR VESSEL POINT NO. 27)

Chinese name:
Duiduan (exchange terminus).
Location:
On the median tubercle of the lip, at the junction of the philtrum and the lip.
Connections:
None.
Direction of strike:
Straight in to the tip of the upper lip.
Damage:
This is a good dim-mak point because it is easy to get to. Its main feature in dim-mak is that it causes shock to the whole system, from the lower lumbar region to the brain, causing mental disorders and confusion. At the very least, it will knock his teeth out!
Set-up point:
Neigwan.
Antidote:
Press down onto Gv 20 and rub Ht 7 downward on the wrist.
Healing:
Innervation is by the buccal branch of the facial nerve and the branch of the infraorbital nerve. Irrigation is by the superior labial artery and vein.

Use for mental disorders, stiffness of the lip, pain in the gums, vomiting, occluded nose, rhinopolypus, seizures, and stomatitis.

Dui means mouth, and *duan* here means tip; the point is at the tip of the upper lip, and its traditional functions are to treat toothache and swollen gums.

To massage, pinch between the thumb and forefinger and press with the fingertip.

Use with St 4, St 5, St 6, St 44, St 45, St 36, Liv 3, Gb 34, Co 4, Co 1, Co 2, Gb 20, and St 12 for stiffness of upper lip.

Use with St 44, St 45, St 41, Co 4, Co 11, Co 1, and Co 2 for pain in the gums.
Applications:
Block his right hook with your left knife edge as your right one-knuckle punch attacks straight in to Gv 27.

GV 28 (GOVERNOR VESSEL POINT NO. 28)

Chinese name:
Yinjiao (gum's junction).

Location:
Between the upper lip and the upper labial gingiva, in the frenulum of the upper lip. *Yin* here refers to the gums, and *jiao* here means to meet; the point is on the incisive suture of the upper gum, where the Cv and the Gv meridians meet.

Connections:
Conceptor vessel.

Direction of strike:
Straight in to the upper lip. Although this point is on the inside of the mouth, you can still get it from the outside. But you will probably also strike to Gv 26.

Damage:
This is not a point I would try to strike; it is on the inside of the mouth, and other points are more dangerous. This is more of a healing point.

Set-up point:
None.

Antidote:
None.

Healing:
Innervation is by the branch of the superior alveolar nerve. Irrigation is by the superior labial artery and vein.

Use for mental disorders, rhinorrhea, pain and swelling of the gums, acute wrist sprain, and rhinopolypus (benign growth from the mucous membrane).

As a point of intersection with the conceptor vessel, its traditional function is to unite the du and ren meridians. It also fixes mental mania and lumbar problems.

To massage, press with fingertips and hold, do rotations clockwise or counterclockwise for xu or shi conditions, and do fingertip percussion.

Use with Cv 24, St 4, Co 4, St 44, St 45, and Ht 8 for ulcers in the mouth.

Use with formula listed under Gv 26 for lockjaw.

Applications:
None.

This brings me to the end of the governor vessel meridian. As you can see, the Gv meridian, like the Cv meridian, has many very dangerous points. Training in Gv and Cv strikes will probably be all that you would ever need for self-defense; in fact, you will probably only ever be able to safely say that you would use four or five of these points automatically in a life-or-death situation.

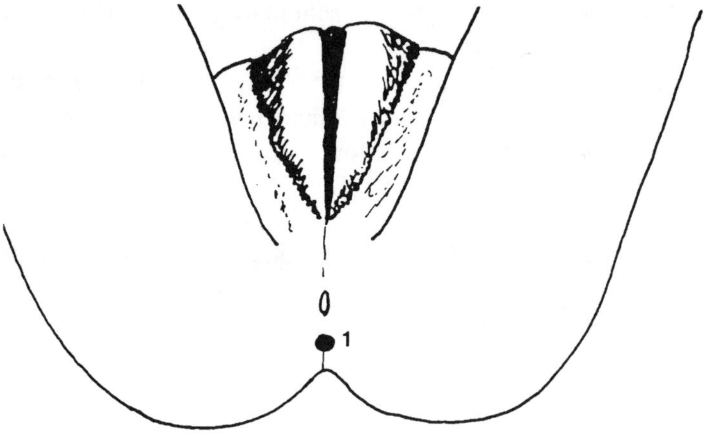

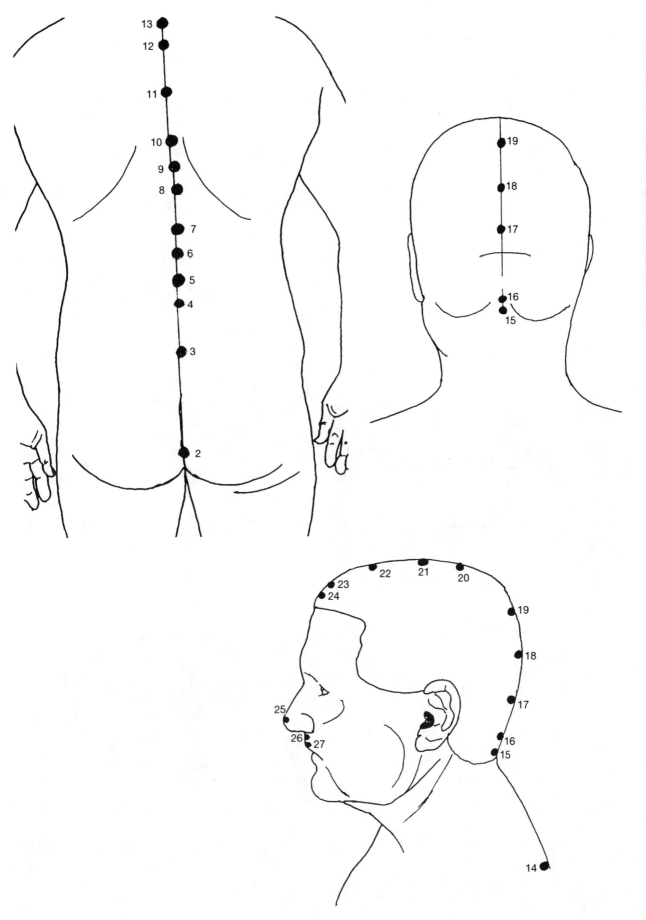

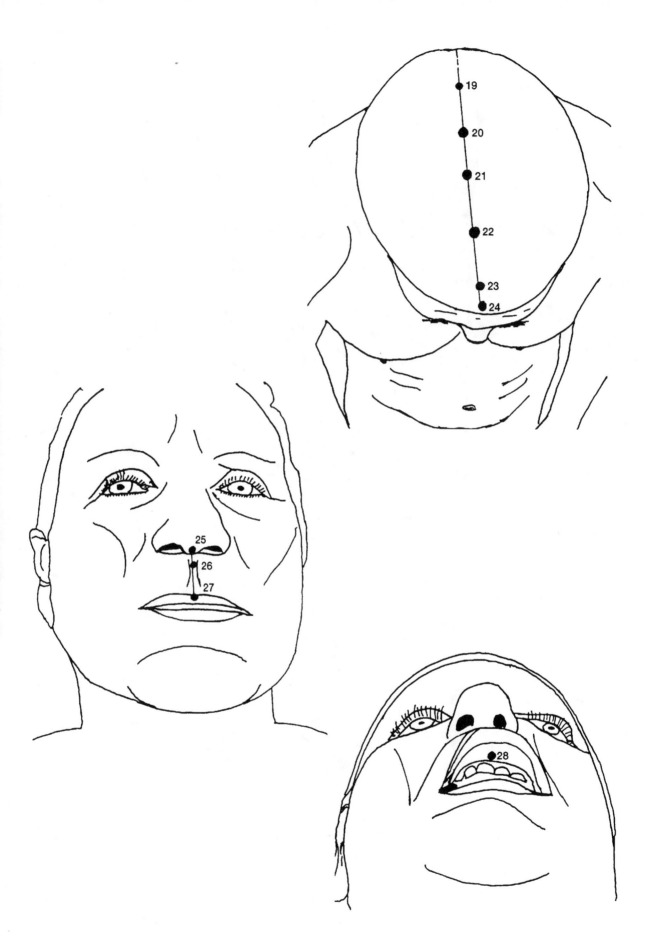

Chapter 3

The Other Extraordinary Meridians and the Extra and New Points

THE SIX OTHER EXTRAORDINARY MERIDIANS

The six other extraordinary meridians have no points of their own, in contrast to the 12 main meridians and the ren and du mai. They are linking meridians that unite all the other meridians. Thus, the individual points of these six are not detailed in this volume because they were covered in depth in the first volume under the main meridians, from which these six other meridians take the names for their points. The dim-mak practitioner is concerned mainly with the points and the combinations of points to strike on each meridian, and the six other meridians are the source of most of the multiple-point strikes. If you take a look at the points on each of these six meridians, you see that they cover several other meridians, linking them together. So, in this chapter, you will learn which combinations of two or three points on the extra meridians to strike for the most deadly multiple strikes. Any of the combinations on the extra meridians will cause death. (Not all of the points are combined, of course; only those that will create the greatest damage are taught.)

It would take a whole book and more to cover the healing, diagnostic, and medical applications of the extraordinary meridians completely, so in this volume some of the healing properties of each are discussed only very briefly.

The Yin Qiao Mai

This meridian is the partner to the ren mai and is regarded as the "guest," while the ren mai is regarded as the "master." Strikes to the yin qiao mai points cause great heat to rise in the body, and the results range from epilepsy to pain in the sexual organs and the upper back to death.

Both the yin and yang qiao mai promote agility (qiao means heel), so in addition to the results of specific combinations, strikes to any of these points individually will make one less agile ("able to jump"). Both of these meridians also dominate the opening and closing of the eyelids, with both circling the eye to enter the brain. Both, then, have a relationship with sleep.

Yin qiao means yin qi, and when the yin qi becomes hyperactive, as with a strike to points on the yin qiao mai, the result will be lassitude and somnolence (weariness and drowsiness) in the recipient. Muscular spasm at the yin aspect of the limbs is also indicated for yin qiao mai strikes.

The points on the yin qiao mai are as follows: Kd 2, Kd 6, Kd 8 (accumulation point), St 9, St 12, and Bl 1. (See the diagrams at the end of this chapter.)

Multiple Strikes on the Yin Qiao Mai

Kd 2 with St 12: This combination of points will cause heat to rise in the brain, resulting in KO and eventual death, both from kidney failure and the loss of the will to live (I was told "not want to live" when taught this combination.) The lower point, on the foot, must be struck a fraction of a second before the upper point. So first Kd 2 is stomped on, and then St 12 must be struck in a downward direction. This combination can also cause epilepsy at some later stage.

Kd 6 with St 9: This combination is again struck with the lower point first. Kd 6 must be struck with a glancing blow downward, and then St 9 must be struck at an angle in toward the backbone. Again, heat rises instantly into the heart, this time causing the heart to race, thus causing high blood pressure and KO and death. This strike will cause great pain in the sexual organs and must be treated by a TCM doctor since Western medicine has no answer other than analgesics.

Kd 8 with Kd 6: These two points can be struck by chopping downward with the heel, first to Kd 8 and then to Kd 6. This will cause instant heavy nausea as a result of the kidneys beginning to fail. Left untreated, it can cause death. Back pain is evident in the long term with this combination.

Kd 8 with Bl 1: This combination is a death-point strike. Strike to Kd 8 first, then to Bl 1, causing massive renal failure. Kd 8 is struck with a glancing blow downwards, and Bl 1 is struck downward.

Kd 8 with St 9 and Bl 1: This is a deadly combination beginning with a strike to Kd 8, then to Bl 1, and finally to St 9, usually with an elbow. Kd 8 is struck downward, Bl 1 is struck downward, and St 9 is struck in the usual way, toward the backbone at a 45-degree angle. Here we get renal as well as heart failure. Revival is not possible.

St 9 with Bl 1: Bl 1 is struck first, followed instantly by St 9. Bl 1 is struck with a one-knuckle punch, slightly in toward the corner of the eye socket, toward the nose, at an angle of 45 degrees. St 9 is struck in toward the backbone at 45 degrees. The head feels as if it will burst, the face goes red, the tongue goes blue, and fainting occurs seconds after this combination strike. It will cause death from heart failure. Revival is not possible.

The Yang Qiao Mai

The yang qiao mai is the "wife" to its partner, the governor vessel meridian, which is regarded as being the "husband." The combinations on this meridian will render effects ranging from lumbar pain to death, with things like epilepsy, hemiplegia, and a tightness of the whole body (tension) in the middle. Strikes to this meridian will generally cause hyperactivity and lack of sleep; the eyes cannot close.

The points on the yang qiao mai are as follows: Bl 1, Gb 20, Bl 62, Bl 61, Bl 59, Si 10, Co 16, Co 15, St 9, St 4, St 3, St 1, and Gb 29. Although some acupuncture texts leave out Gb 20 as a yang qiao mai point, I was taught to include it. For the sake of convenience, the points on the yang qiao mai are usually shown in a straight line from foot to head. However, these points shunt all over the body jumping over some points and going back to them later. For dim-mak, this is not important, however, since we are given the combinations of points to strike.

Multiple Strikes on the Yang Qiao Mai

Bl 62 with Gb 29: This combination of points struck consecutively, the Bl 62 point first, will paralyze the leg, causing the recipient to fall down. The Bl 62 point must be struck by stomping on it, whereas the Gb 29 point must be struck straight in. You might block his left attack with your right palm, followed by a stomp onto Bl 62. Your left palm can take over the block (not that you need to, as the stomp, if struck right on the point, will end the attack) while your right one-knuckle punch attacks straight in to Gb 29.

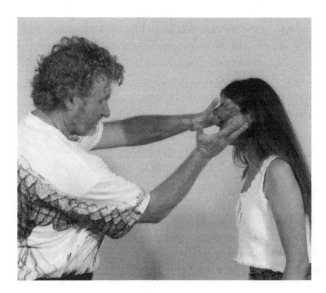

Figure 320

Si 10 with St 9 and Gb 29: This triple strike will cause death. Si 10 must be struck first, followed by St 9 and Gb 29. The combination causes extreme qi drainage. The recipient feels immediate drowsiness, followed by an irregular heartbeat, which causes great weakness and nausea and then death. Execute a simple slam into Si 10 with the right palm as he attacks with a left straight, for instance, then turn your waist to the right as your left palm attacks to St 9 and your right knee attacks to Gb 29.

St 1 with St 4 and St 9: This combination is also deadly. If you leave out the St 9 strike, it will cause such great nausea that the recipient will have to be hospitalized because it causes fainting spells. St 1 and St 4 are struck almost at the same time, St 1 coming first. You can use both knife edges to respond to his left arm attack, for instance, by striking to neigwan and Lu 8. This will cause qi drainage to begin with. Then both knife edges come back across to St 1 and St 4 (fig. 320). Then you turn your waist back to your right as your left palm strikes into St 9. This is death.

St 3 with St 9: This combination causes extreme nausea and vomiting, followed by blackout and death. St 3 is struck first, followed closely by St 9. You could use the same hand to strike to these two points. For instance, he could attack with a right straight or hook. Your left palm slams into his right neigwan as your right index and longest fingers strike upward into both St 3 points just under his cheekbone. Your waist now rebounds to your right, thus loading your right knife edge, then turns to your left to lead your right knife edge into his right St 9 point.

St 1 with Gb 20: This is a devastating double strike, used mainly when you have closed with the attacker, as in the case of grappling while still standing. The left or right side of your forehead strikes into his St 1 point just under his eye, followed very closely by your thumb-side knife-edge strike into Gb 20. Your palm, of course, has to be around behind his neck to do this, and it will be if you are grappling. This strike causes death if Gb 20 is struck hard enough. At the very least it will knock him out.

Co 16 with St 1: Co 16 is struck first, followed closely by St 1. In a grappling situation, for instance, you can access Co 16 with your elbow, hammering straight down onto the shoulder near the neck, then headbutt his St 1 point. This combination is designed to cause extreme nausea, stopping the fight. It is a good combination to use when you do not wish to kill someone but only to end the confrontation, for example.

I have covered most of the more deadly combinations on this meridian; of course, there are others. If you use St 9 with any of the other points on this meridian, death is not far off. The lower leg points combined with any of the St points, except St 9, will cause great local pain and nausea.

The Chong Mai

Chong means "vital," and in dim-mak we consider this the "life force" meridian. Strikes to multiple points on this meridian will cause death. The chong mai is the "father," while the yin wei mai is the "mother."

The course of the chong mai runs in three lines. The common line goes from around Cv 1 or the uterus, descends, and emerges from the perineum to divide into the three branches. The first branch goes from the perineum, curves around the anus, and enters the vertebral column; hence the channel's other name of "life force meridian." The second branch goes around the external genitals, bifurcates, and follows both sides of the kidney meridian. It then goes from the neck to the mouth and ascends to the infraorbital region. The third branch also divides in two and descends the medial aspects of the lower limbs, to the heel and through the medial malleolus. A divergent branch passes through the dorsum of the foot to end up between the great and second toes.

This meridian regulates the blood and qi of the 12 main meridians; it is often called "the sea of the 12 main meridians." It regulates the menstrual flow and the ascending and descending of qi in the body. When this meridian is diseased, stagnation of the qi will occur, as well as disorders of the reproductive system. In females, when the qi and blood of the chong mai are abundant, menstrual flow will begin at around age 14. This is because of the strong chong mai, which also strengthens the ren mai and the sexual urge. At around age 49, the chong mai becomes weaker until menstrual flow stops. Qigong is one practice that will help the chong mai remain strong. It is indicated in men with a lesser sexual urge and less blood to the yong muscle (penis) (in other words, they find it harder to get it up—I guess many people will be now taking up qigong and trying to heal their kidney jing!).

The chong mai has a great effect upon the stomach and the hormones. For instance, in ancient texts, theories such as the Nanjing Extraordinary Vessel Theory tell us that a eunuch does not have hair around his mouth or lips because he has had his penis and testicles cut off. In this case the chong mai cannot nourish the mouth. The chong mai is also dependent upon the kidney jing, so this indicates the interrelationship between the kidneys and the chong mai. (In fact, all of the meridians have some interrelationship and depend upon each other in some way for their power to either heal or harm the body.)

In dim-mak, the chong mai either runs through or very close to the kidney channel up the front of the abdomen. And it is the combination of kidney points that makes it so dangerous. Add its beginning point of St 30 and you also get stomach problems. Strikes to the backbone are also very dangerous because of the first branch of this meridian, the internal pathway of which passes to the three yin foot meridians and has no points along it. On the charts, however, it is customary to show only the line of the meridian where there are points.

The chong mai runs from St 30 to Cv 1 to Kd 11 to Kd 21, then it travels down to the three yin foot meridians. This small meridian is very important in Chinese medicine, but there is some argument as to exactly where it runs and what it does. In dim-mak, however, we are very clear on the point combinations and their effects.

Multiple Strikes on the Chong Mai

Kd 20 and Kd 21 with St 30: Both kidney points can be struck at the same time with the one hand, and then the St 30 point can be struck straight in with either the palm or the knee. The kidney points must be struck first, though. These points must be struck quite hard, or nothing will happen. Otherwise, the combination will cause death either immediately or up to three hours later.

Kd 21 with Cv 1 and Kd 16: At most, this combination will cause the heart to stop, resulting in death. At least it will cause severe muscle tension, especially in the upper back, and continual diarrhea. Mental illness is also apparent with this strike. To get at the three points is not easy, however, as you must strike in the correct order of Kd 21, Cv 1, and then Kd 16. You could strike to Kd 21 using your left palm, followed by your knee up into Cv 1 and your right palm to Kd 16.

Kd 14 with Kd 21: This is a death-point strike if struck really hard. A mild strike will cause KO. You strike Kd 14 first, perhaps using a right palm, followed by your left palm in to Kd 21. This technique is covered in the taiji old yang form by the posture known as "double dragon strike" and is also included in most karate katas.

If you put any of the chong mai kidney points with St 30 or Cv 1, you will have devastating multiple strikes. There are many combinations, but for the sake of reality, the above are the ones I teach.

The Yin Wei Mai

The yin wei mai is the "mother" and partner to the chong mai. As far as dim-mak is concerned, some of the most deadly combinations are on this meridian, such as Cv 22 and Liv 14. These multiple strikes will cause anything from dizziness to death, with the following in between: chest (heart) pain, vomiting, diarrhea, digestion problems, liver and gallbladder pain, KO, weakness from diaphragm damage, pain below the sternum, nosebleed (relating to the lungs), joint pain, uncoordination of the limbs, and the list goes on.

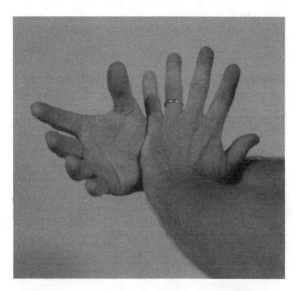

Figure 321

Wei means to connect, and the yin meridians connect to the yin wei mai. Strikes to both yin and yang wei mai generally result in trouble with the balance of yin and yang in the whole body. When these two meridians are working normally, there is balance between yin and yang in the body. When the yin wei mai is damaged, the recipient will have general heart pain, gastric pain, and pain of the chest and abdomen. The points on the yin wei mai are as follows: Kd 9, Sp 13, Sp 15, Sp 16, Liv 14, Cv 22, and Cv 23.

Multiple Strikes on the Yin Wei Mai

Kd 9 with Cv 17 and Sp 13: This will drain the lower heater of qi, causing weakness in the lower body and legs. It will also damage the kidney jing, causing overall weakness throughout the whole body. You must strike Kd 9 first. A method to access this combination would be to block his oncoming attack and then strike with a glancing blow downward to Kd 9 with your heel, then slam him in the middle of the chest at Cv 17, bringing your knee up into Sp 13.

Sp 13 with Liv 14: This is a death combination, causing the body to go into convulsions, which results in heart stoppage. Sp 13 must be struck first. The direction for Sp 13 is straight in and slightly toward the centerline, while the direction for Liv 14 is straight in. To access this strike, first we would perhaps block both of his attacking arms (as in the case of a grappler attacking) on the inside of his forearms at both neigwans. Then your left palm is placed on the inside of your right wrist, the left palm being yin shaped while the right is yang-shaped. Your left palm is facing downward while the right is facing toward you. Squeeze both of your elbows together, thrusting out both of your palms with great power into Sp 13. The left palm is helping the right palm. The left palm has released its yang qi by changing shape to a flexed palm, while the right palm has released its yin qi by changing state to a rounded shape (limp), as in

Figure 322

Figure 321. Now, rebound up into Liv 14 using the same strike, loading and releasing exactly as in the previous strike to Sp 13, only end up at Liv 14 (fig. 322). The waist is the power for this strike.

Liv 14 with Cv 22 and Cv 23: You do not need to use Cv 23; the other two by themselves result in death. However, the three points together are indicated as the strike. Liv 14 is struck first, followed by Cv 22 and then Cv 23. The directions are all straight in, with Cv 23 being aimed slightly upward. This series of strikes causes death through suffocation and heart stoppage, with no revival likely.

Sp 15 and Sp 13: This double strike causes severe lower heater problems with qi drainage and weakness of the whole body. Sp 15 is struck first, and both points are struck straight in. Extreme dizziness and vomiting are also apparent with this strike. You could use the double dragon strike mentioned earlier here.

The above are the point combinations I teach on the yin wei mai. There are obviously more combinations, causing lesser effects than death, but I wouldn't advise experimenting with these in the training hall or seminar, for instance, just to see if they work. To do so would be irresponsible.

The Yang Wei Mai

In its relationship to the dai mai, the yang wei mai is "female." We can cause anything from dizziness to KO to death by using the combinations on this meridian. You will notice that there are many Gb points on the yang wei mai, and a KO usually occurs just before death with many of these. We also have Th points that are dangerous all by themselves.

This meridian controls the external parts of the body, and if it is damaged, the body is open to external syndromes of cold or heat. When this meridian is damaged, the recipient will have fevers, aversion to cold, etc.

The points on the yang wei mai are as follows: Bl 57, Bl 63, Gb 35, Gb 29, Co 14, Th 13, Th 15, Gb 21, Si 10, Gb 20, Gb 19, Gb 18, Gb 17, Gb 16, Gb 15, Gb 14, Gb 13, Gb 15, and Gv 16. The combinations here are endless, so I will only give the ones that I know and teach.

Multiple Strikes on the Yang Wei Mai

Gb 35 and Gb 29: These will cause KO with leg paralysis. Strike to Gb 35 downward with the heel, and then strike straight in to Gb 29 using, perhaps, the knee.

Co 14 with Gb 21 and Th 13: This combination will cause KO at most or severe qi drainage at least. It will also have long-term effects upon the recipient's ability to take in "earth qi," causing emotional and physical problems later in life. Co 14 must be struck first, straight in, while Gb 21 is struck downward onto the shoulder. Th 13 can be struck at the same time as Co 14 with the palm because of the close proximity of the two points. You could block his left attack from the outside over to your left with your right palm, bringing that same palm back to strike straight in to Co 14 and Th 13; then the elbow is able to strike downward onto Gb 21 (or if the attacker is too tall, use the palm or knife edge).

Co 14 with Gb 20: This combination is deadly, because it causes brain confusion and severe qi drainage followed by KO and heart stoppage. In this case the heart is very hard to restart, even with CPR. You must strike Co 14 first, straight in to the shoulder, followed by an upward strike to Gb 20 at the base of the skull. This combination is easy to access from a grappling-type situation. You could close and strike him at Co 14 using the thumb knuckle, followed by a strike to Gb 20 using the reverse knife edge of your other palm.

Gb 14 with Gb 20: Again, this is a very deadly strike since it sends a rush of qi to the head, which causes the body to give up its natural defenses before the strike to Gb 20 causing KO and/or death. Gb 14 must be struck upward only in this instance, and Gb 20 must be struck upward as well.

Tw 15 with Gb 19: Th 15 combined with Gb 19 is a death strike. The Th 15 strike upsets the balance of yin and yang in the body when Gb 19 is struck straight after. The Gb 19 shot will kill, especially when struck after the Th 15 shot. You must strike Th 15 straight in first, followed by Gb 19 straight in to the back of the ear, either using a one-knuckle punch or a palm-heel strike.

Again, there are obviously many other combinations. Generally, though, if you use one of the yang wei mai Gb points with any other yang wei mai points, you have a very dangerous multiple strike.

The Dai Mai

The dai mai (girdle meridian) is the male to the yang wei mai. Dai mai points can be used all by themselves as excellent set-up points or in combination with other points as quite deadly multiple-point strikes. The point combinations, or even single points, will always cause a dissociation between heaven and earth or man and God. The result of such strikes is that the upper body does not know what the lower body is doing. The dai mai points will also weaken the legs instantly. The dai mai controls all the other meridians by loosening or tightening; it is like a belt going around the girdle area (the dai character in the Chinese language means belt). It is the only meridian that runs transversely across the surface of the body. Its general functions are to bind up the other meridians and to control leukorrhea in females. Strikes to the dai mai will cause general weakness in the lower back and waist, excessive leukorrhea, and, in the long term, distension of the abdomen, prolapse of the uterus, and weakness of the waist. The points on the dai mai are Liv 13, Gb 26, Gb 27, and Gb 28. It is only a short meridian, but it makes up for this in its potency in the dim-mak area.

Multiple Strikes on the Dai Mai

Liv 13 with Gv 26: This combination is a death-point strike. Liv 13 is struck first straight in, followed by a strike to Gb 26 straight in from the side. Liv 13 is usually struck with the tips of the fingers, while Gb 26 is struck with the palm heel. You could strike both of the attacker's arms at the neigwan points as he attacks with two hands. Both of your palms now attack to Liv 13 and Gb 26 respectively (fig. 323).

Liv 13 with Gb 27: This strike is also death. You can now reverse the hands so that the right tips of your fingers go into Liv 13 on his left side while your left palm strikes to Gb 27. You could use the same method of attack as the last method. Liver failure and heart stoppage are the results of this strike.

Gb 26 with Gb 28: This combination will cause so much brain confusion that the recipient is likely to go insane. His upper body will be doing things that the lower body is not aware of (e.g., his mind will be thinking that the legs are moving forward when they might be stepping backward). You can access these points with one palm at the same time; this is one of the few combinations where the points do not need to be struck individually. Or you could drop your knee onto both of these points, once you have thrown the attacker to the ground, with devastating results.

It is my idea that if you are going to use the extraordinary meridians, then you must make a specialty out of using them. Make them your favorite techniques, as you can get extremely good results in the dim-mak area just using the points of the extra meridians.

Figure 323

THE EXTRA AND NEW POINTS

The extra and new points are those that do not seem to lie on any particular meridian and those that have been discovered in relatively modern times. Perhaps in the future someone will discover that there are other meridians that link all of these points. There are anywhere between 30 to 1,500 extra and new points in the body, depending upon which text you read. Many are right over main points, and the names of these points differ in many texts. Many of them are so close to mainstream points that it is not worth including them with reference to dim-mak. Others are, for example, inside the mouth or ear. So I will only be including those few extra and new points that I have been taught and have had experience with and know to work as written. You will see that many of these points are struck when you strike many of the main points anyway, so it is difficult to judge which point is actually doing the damage.

I will try to keep these points grouped in their areas of the body since it can become confusing otherwise. The only way we have to recognize the extra and new points is by their Chinese names, which in most cases reflect either a physical location or the point's function in the healing area.

Sishencong

Located on the top of the head, there are four points that make up this group of points. They are also sometimes called "the inner square" in dim-mak. *Si* means a group of four points—front, back, left, and right; *shen* means spirit or mind, and *cong* means to cause one to be smart or intelligent. If you find bahui, or Gv 20, and take points on the four points of the compass 1 cun distance from it, then you have this square of points surrounding bahui.

In dim-mak, the strike to sishencong is done with the whole palm slapping downward onto the top of the head, striking all five points (including bahui) at the same time.

This strike will cause extreme dizziness, with insomnia as a long-term effect. It is also indicated to cause mental instability.

In the healing area it is good for mental activity and to sharpen the intelligence.

Yintang

Meaning "decorating place," this is the point that people used to decorate for cosmetic reasons. Yin means to stain, and tang means an area or place. It is located at the third eye point, and in fact is the third eye point between the eyebrows on the Gv meridian, but is not a Gv point.

In dim-mak, this point is usually used with a cupped slap to the side of the neck, causing KO, and is in fact the old "evangelist's knockout." Those who can knock people out and are not setting up the whole thing at seminars and so on always place their other hand at the side of the neck first and then push backward onto yintang. It shocks the brain, causing KO. It is usually struck using the "mounts" of the fingers, which are pushed out (protruded) as the palm makes contact with the point.

In the healing area this point is used for things like vertigo, pain in the eye, red eyes, nausea, vomiting, and acute infantile convulsions. It can be combined with neigwan for things like seasickness and nausea, and it is often bled.

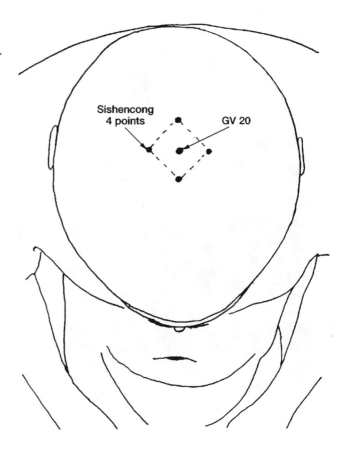

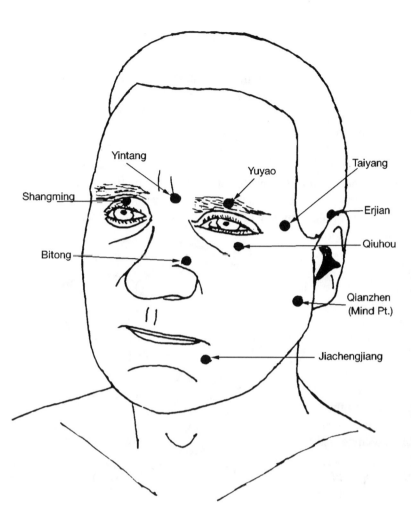

Labels on diagram: Yintang, Yuyao, Taiyang, Shangming, Erjian, Qiuhou, Bitong, Qianzhen (Mind Pt.), Jiachengjiang

Yuyao

Meaning the "fish's belly," this point is located in the middle of each eyebrow. It is struck straight in with a one-knuckle punch, causing considerable damage to the qi system of the body by draining qi. In the healing area it is used for painful eyes, eyelids that flicker, and mouth and eyes awry.

Taiyang

This point is so close to Gb 1 at the corner of the eye that it is impossible to miss it when striking to Gb 1. It also is struck from rear to front, causing KO and internal yang qi damage, resulting in weakness. It is struck with the same weapons that Gb 1 is struck with, such as a finger strike moving from rear to front. It means "supreme" (as in t'ai from t'ai chi ch'uan, or supreme ultimate boxing) yang, because this is where the yang meridians converge and where the yang qi is the most abundant. In the healing area is it used for things like trigeminal neuralgia, eye problems, and one-sided headache. It can also be used with Gb 20 for squinting eyes.

Qianzhen

Meaning "to pull normal," this point is also called the "mind point" in dim-mak, as it causes KO by blocking the messages from the central nervous system (CNS) to the brain. Many boxers have been struck on this point, and even with the gloves it causes them to fall down. It is located 0.5 cun anterior to the lobulus auriculae, which means just in front of the earlobe on the back part of the jaw. It is a particularly sore point when pressed back and in toward the backbone. It is usually struck with a one-knuckle punch, or you can use a palm heel.

In healing, it is used for halitosis, sore rear teeth, mouth and eyes awry, and ulcers in the mouth.

Striking this point could also cause KO because the brain stem is kinked when the head moves backward violently. This kind of KO is prevalent in boxing when a strike of great power hits the chin area anywhere, causing the brain stem to be kinked.

Yiming (New Point)

This point is located just back from Th 17, 1 cun toward the backbone. When Th 17 is struck, it is likely that this point is also struck. However, the direction for yiming is straight in, whereas the direction for Th 17 is from rear to front. It is usually struck with a one-knuckle punch and has a devastating effect on the brain, causing KO or even death.

Meaning "eye bright," its healing functions are related to the eyes, causing them to be brighter, improving eyesight, and treating night blindness, early signs of glaucoma, tinnitus, vertigo, hysteria, and mania.

Anmian

Meaning "sound sleep," this is what this point does with regard to healing. It is situated midway between Th 17 and Gb 20. This is a death point all by itself, but include either Gb 20 or Th 17 and revival is impossible. The strike is done in toward the base of the brain, hence its danger. It will cause extreme dizziness at least, KO somewhere in between, and acute insomnia in the long term.

The healing benefits of this point are insomnia, dream-disturbed sleep, headache, vertigo, palpitation, hypertension, deafness, and hysteria. Massage toward Th 17 using the thumb.

Erjian

Meaning "apex of the ear," this point is situated directly above the apex of the ear on the side of the skull. Extreme dizziness and imbalance will occur when this point is struck straight in toward the skull. It will cause KO at least and death at most. Combine this point with any of the gallbladder points around the ear, and you indeed have a devastating combination of point strikes.

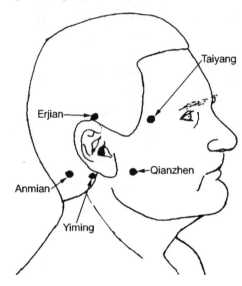

In the healing area, this point is good for sore and red eyes, sty, sore throat, and corneal opacity. It is used traditionally to brighten the eyes, dispel pathogenic wind, and stop pain. It can be used with Gv 15 for sore throat and aphonia.

Qiuhou

Meaning "behind the eyeball," this point is located just under the eye in a line with the outer edge of the pupil. It is used to heal eye diseases. This point is usually struck with a one-knuckle punch slightly downward into the lower eye socket, causing obvious damage because of its location by the eye. Even when struck lightly, this point will cause great throbbing pain for days afterward. This strike will stop any fight when executed correctly.

Bitong

When struck here, the recipient feels great nausea and weakness in the whole body due to this point's action upon the lungs. Great local pain and qi drainage are felt when bitong is struck with a one-knuckle punch at an angle of 45 degrees to the side of the nose.

Shangming

This point is located in the middle of the upper eyelid (if the eyelid is closed) or on the superior aspect of the eyeball if the eyes are open. To strike it is to strike to the eyes with obvious results. No one can carry on when this point has been struck; the pain is just too great, and apart from that, you cannot see! Shang means superior, and ming means brightening. In the healing area, it can improve the eyesight. Other healing applications include ametropia, optic atrophy, redness in the eye, and excessive lacrimation.

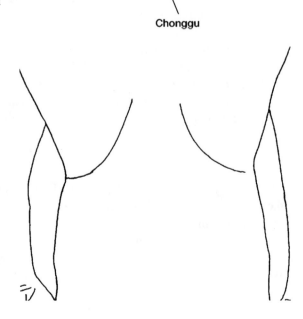

Jiachengjiang

Jia means lateral or beside, and *chengjiang* means Cv 24. Striking this point, located 1 cun lateral to Cv 24, just back from the tip of the jaw, does obvious damage to the chin, causing the mind to black out for a few seconds, resulting in both KO and jaw damage. It must be struck at a slight angle inward to the jaw. Some of its healing benefits are facial paralysis, ulceration of the gum, spasm of the face, and trigeminal neuralgia.

Chonggu

Meaning "respected bone," chonggu refers to C7 (cervical 7). The point is located just to the side of and between the spinous process of C6 and C7. It is a good point to strike to should the attacker have his back toward you. It can also be accessed from the front, as in the case of grappling with one hand around over the back of the neck. This strike also attacks the yang, causing extreme drowsiness and/or mental instability.

The healing benefits are common cold, asthma, cough, maniacal behavior with emotional excitement, insanity and emotional depression, pulmonary tuberculosis, neck rigidity, and swollen neck with difficulty swallowing.

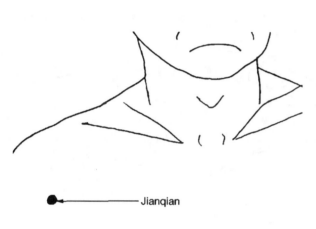

Jianqian

Jianqian

Meaning "shoulder anterior," jianqian can be used with Sp 19 to affect what the opposite leg does. It takes power from that leg, as well as causing great local pain. So a strike here just before an opposite leg attack will cause that leg to become weak. We can also use this point when we intend to strike to points that would cause the attacker to sit back onto the rear leg, for instance, which will be weak and not able to hold his weight after this point strike. It is located at the midpoint of the line connecting the upper end of the anterior axillary crease and Co 15. It is usually struck straight in.

Healing applications of this point are motor impairment, frozen shoulder (can be used with Ht 1 for this), paralysis of the upper limbs, and pain in the shoulder.

Bizhong

Bizhong is, I am told, an excellent point to use with Lu 5. If Lu 5 is struck straight in, then the palm is allowed to slide down the arm (with force) over bizhong and the next points, called erbai. I have not had direct experience with these points; however, I am told that they will cause a KO. My guess is that it is really the strike to the qi-draining Lu 5 that does the work.

Meaning "center of the forearm," this point is located between the transverse crease of the wrist and that of the elbow between the radius and ulna. Healing indications include pain in the forearm, paralysis of the upper limbs, hysteria, and hypochondriac pain.

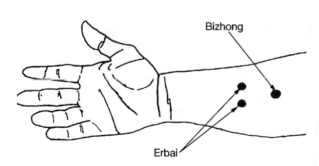

Bizhong

Erbai

Erbai

These two points are located 4 cun above the transverse crease of the wrist, on either side of the tendon of the muscle flexor carpi radialis. Both points are at the same level. *Er* means two, and *bai* means white, which means that these points have to be understood to be used. They have special indications, and the practitioner must know about these in order to treat using them. These points are used with bizhong and also with Lu 5 to cause a KO. However, they can also be used all by themselves as very potent arm damaging points when struck straight in using a knife-edge strike. Great local pain and qi drainage are indicated.

The healing properties of these points are for hypochondriac pain, prolapse of the rectum, hemorrhoids, and painful forearm.

Yaotongxue (New Point)

Yaotong means lumbar pain, and *xue* means point. It is also called lumbago point. There are three of these points on the back of the hand about one and a half cun distal to zhongquan and the same distance between each other. These points also create much pain and local qi drainage when struck with a backfist. These are also good set-up points. In healing, these points are punctured 0.8 cun deep toward the center of the palm. The patient is also advised to do some lumbar rotations while the needles are still in situation.

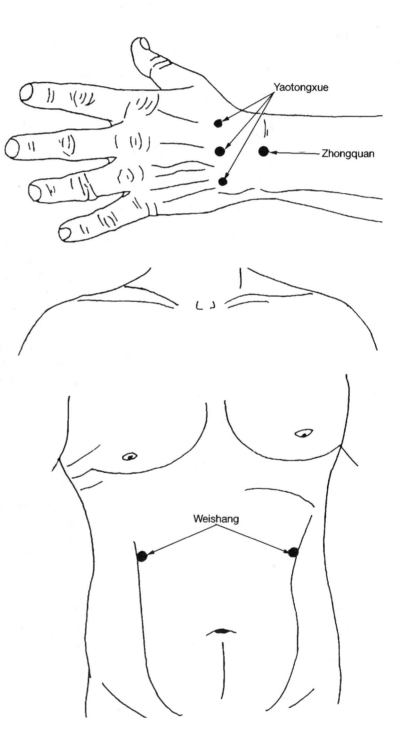

Zhongquan

Zhongquan means dorsum and spring or depression. Hence this point is located right in the middle of the back of the wrist flexure, midway along a line drawn between Co 5 and Th 4. When it is struck straight in with perhaps a backfist, there is extreme local pain hence qi drainage. This gives plenty of time to execute a more deadly attack. It is a nice set-up point strike.

The healing properties of this extra point are abdominal distension and pain, fullness and distension of the hypochondriac region, cough, asthma, and epigastric pain.

Weishang

Meaning stomach lifting, this point is located at either side of the waist where the waist is smallest. It is 2 cun above the navel and 4 cun lateral on both sides. It is used to lift the stomach in the case of prolapsed stomach. It can also treat gastroptosis. When struck on either side, this point has the ability to kill, sending a shock wave up into the lungs and heart, and it can rupture the internal organs that lie behind it. Usually it is struck on both sides at the same time with two palm strikes. Your opponent is in great danger should you also strike to Liv 13 on both sides because it is quite close to this point.

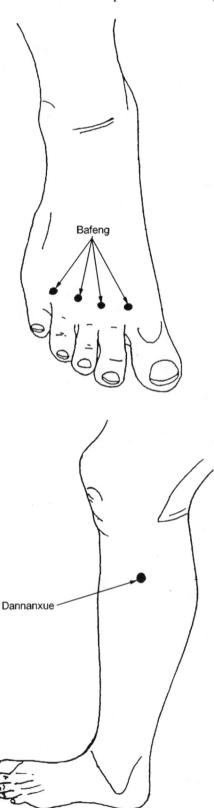

Bafeng

Ba means eight, as in bagwazhang—and in this case it refers to the eight spaces between the 10 toes—while *feng* means the pathogenic wind. The eight points are located on the junction of the red and white skin on the webs of the toes.

Used for healing, these points will eliminate pathogenic wind, ease pain, activate blood circulation, and remove obstructions from the meridians. A peculiar use of this point is in the treatment of snake bite. However, I don't think I would trust this method of treatment here in Australia, where we have the world's most deadly snakes—one of which, the fierce snake, can kill 250,000 mice with one drop of its poison. This point is also used for toothache, cyanosis, and menstrual disorders.

When stomped on, these points cause great local pain and qi drainage. Drop a hammer on your foot near this area and see how it hurts; you just have to sit down, the pain is so great.

There are many extra points on the hand and fingers, but for dim-mak these are not practical. For instance, you can exert some considerable pain by pressing onto the baxie points in between the knuckles, but this pain would not suffice to bring anyone to his knees in a realistic situation. They work fine in demonstration, where someone has given you his hand and you apply pressure to see him flinch, but in a realistic, life-threatening situation this would not work. First you would have to get at his hand, and in that time he has knifed you. It's the same with locks and holds—these work fine in controlled situations, such as in class or at a seminar, where the participant gives you his hand. But try getting a lock or hold on in a realistic situation and you risk your life! I have always said that if you wish to use locks and holds, hit him first, then get the lock to control him. In my considerable years of training, no one has ever been able to get any kind of lock on me when I did not wish them to. And I always tell my own students that if anyone is able to get a lock on them, then they should go find another teacher because I am not doing my job.

Dannangxue (New Point)

Dannang means gallbladder, and *xue* means point; this point is situated near Gb 34, about 1 to 2 cun below that point on the gallbladder meridian. The point is movable, as so many of the acupuncture points are. So with most of the points, using a larger weapon such as a palm strike will ensure that the strike hits the target. Where I have indicated a smaller weapon, these points do not usually move. A hard strike here will cause qi drainage and even KO when struck really hard straight in with perhaps a heel. The point is quite sore to the touch.

In healing, this point is used for acute and chronic cholecystitis (inflammation of the gallbladder). It is very useful at the onset of this ailment.

Luozhen

I mention this point because it is excellent for healing neck sprain, something that martial artists get often while training incorrectly! When struck, it sends something that feels like an electric shock up the arm and down the hand, causing qi drainage. It is located back from the index finger's web. Meaning "neck sprain," luozhen is located about .5 cun back from the metacarpophalangeal joint. It is sometimes called wailaogong. In addition to neck strain, it also helps with acute gastric pain, painful shoulder, and pain in the arm.

The above are the points that I teach and recommend. There are, however, literally thousands more extra and new points. I would suggest that if you are interested in the extra and new points, go and purchase one of the few good books on the subject. I have indicated only those that I know to have a dim-mak effect. There are others that also have a dim-mak effect but are located, for instance, between the toes!

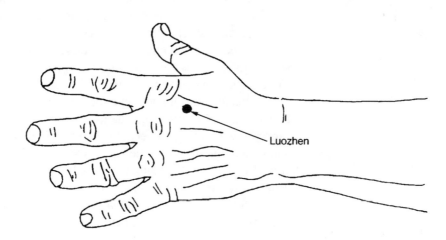

Luozhen

Chapter 4

The Best Strikes and Points

Obviously, it would be impossible for anyone to learn all of the dim-mak points and be able to use them in a fighting situation. And it is not just a matter of hitting anywhere and hoping for the best, because many of the points do not respond—aside from purely physical damage locally—to anything but qi disruptive strikes with intent. Furthermore, many of them must be struck exactly on the point and in the correct direction if they are to have any effect other than purely physical (e.g., a broken bone).

So in this chapter, I will give my advice on which points are the best ones to train in. As you read, keep in mind that although some points might be quite dangerous, they might be located, for instance, under the foot, offering no way of actually accessing them in a life-or-death situation. Others, such as St 9, can be activated at seminars where the instructor will pick out a sitting duck and strike to the point to cause a dramatic KO. But like all of the points, this one requires a solid background in a martial system that advocates streetwise fighting if it is to be used effectively in a self-defense situation. You can train all your life in striking to St 9 point and never be able to use it because you do not know how to fight!

When I say "know how to fight," I do not mean training in karate or gung-fu or jujutsu for 20 years. I mean, really knowing how to fight in the street, which, of course, is totally different than "fighting" in the dojo. A martial art is not automatically a system of self-defense or fighting; it has to be turned into self-defense with the addition of things like fa-jing (explosive energy), reflex movements, and, most of all, timing. These things are not taught in martial arts systems; they are add-ons learned later, once you have learned the basic martial system.

Many martial artists have raised the question of why we don't see people dropping like flies in so-called full-contact tournaments or boxing matches, since there are so many points to strike. (There are no full-contact tournaments by the way.) In many tournaments, for instance, the participants are allowed to punch to the chest area but not to the face, and there are many deadly points all over the chest area.

The answer is simple. In the case of the martial art tournaments, the attackers simply do not know how to punch! I have taught some very highly ranked karate people, and this has been my general observation.

The old reverse punch, for instance, considered by many to be the most powerful of all karate-type punches, is not that great in reality. When I demonstrate "iron shirt," a technique whereby one can build up a defense around the whole midsection, I always pick my mark. First I see how the workshop participants are punching, and then I pick out the person who is doing typical karate-type punching to punch me in the midsection with his best reverse punch. Invariably, it does nothing at all. This is nothing special, just a simple training method. If, however, I see that someone is using fa-jing punching, then I will not pick that person.

In typical karate-type punching (and I say "typical" because there are some schools that have seen the light and are now training in more substantial punching methods), the energy is blocked at the shoulder, and only physical damage can be done. The points around where an attack is aimed are not affected because there is no "adverse qi" going into them. I have demonstrated this by having a workshop participant strike someone on the head using, for instance, a hammer fist (lightly, of course, so that damage is not done to the person receiving the blow). Usually, nothing happens, just some discomfort. Then I strike with the same physical power but use a fa-jing punch with adverse qi flowing, and the result is great pain and leg buckling. (There are some simple training methods to gain this fa-jing, which are covered on some of my training tapes.)

In the case of boxing, the hand is covered with padding, and it would take a very well-placed strike to actually strike a point. The mind point is one that can be accessed when wearing boxing gloves. This happened in one of three-time world champion Jeff Fenech's matches when he struck his opponent with a right cross to the "mind point," sending him to the mat. Fenech himself was surprised, I believe, judging by the look on his face. The commentators were also stunned. But I saw immediately that the strike, even with the gloves on, went right into the "mind point," causing a KO.

There are many points that will work no matter how you strike them—even if you are in an accident, for example, and they are struck somehow. Points such as St 9 or Cv 14 will work every time, no matter what punch you are using. When my son was seven years old, he could knock me out with a blow to triple heater 23 (Th 23). But 75 percent of the points must be struck using fa-jing and adverse qi in order to get the effects that I write about.

The pressure and tension of a real fight will cause you to lose 90 percent of your technique—technique that may have taken you 20 years to gather. So in teaching people self-defense, I endeavor to give them the 10 percent that will save them in a real situation by using dim-mak, fa-jing, and the reptile brain.

People always ask me what points I use and train in. This is okay for me, and it serves as a guide so that you can at least take what I have learned through experience and be fairly confident that these points will also work for you. But you must also discover what points suit you best and then work in only those points and methods of accessing those points.

I only have a handful of points that I train in myself, and these are the ones that I regard as the most deadly. For a point to be considered as such takes more than its being dangerous because it has a devastating effect on the human anatomy; ease of access and ease of use also have to be taken into account. So, for instance, if a very deadly point is in back of the attacker, sure, you can use it, given certain circumstances and/or methods, but this point is not easy to get at, so its position on the deadly scale might be lower than a technically less deadly point that is much easier to get at.

The following four points are the ones I teach at one-day seminars for law enforcement officers. They are those that will work every time, are easy to access, and are very deadly.

Figure 324

STOMACH 9 (ST 9)

St 9 causes death instantly, is very easy to get at, and offers extremely easy methods of access, so this point is probably the highest on my list of dangerous points. It is the one that I teach my children to use in a dangerous situation. This point will work every time by causing either KO or death as a result of heart stoppage. All you have to do is raise the knife edge of one hand to access it. Or you can block an oncoming attack with your left palm while you thrust the right knife edge into St 9 (fig. 324). It can be used in a situation where, for instance, a small child has been abducted and is being carried off. It is relatively easy to get a palm into this point, and even though the child is small and lacks the power of an adult, the effect of KO will be apparent (figs. 325 and 326).

You can use many different weapons to gain access to this point. The elbow can be used with devastating results—just move in a little closer after the above shot and rebound into an elbow strike to St 9. It can also be accessed during a chokeout or a sleeper hold. It can be accessed with a punch or a strike with the tips of the fingers. Or, to access the side of his neck opposite that shown in the above photo (fig. 324), use a reverse knife-edge strike or thrust the back of your palm into the point.

STOMACH 5 (ST 5)

This is one of my favorite points because it is easy to get to and works like a charm to knock out your adversary. You can either use a punch to the side of the jaw or a palm strike. I prefer the palm strike since you do not have to be that accurate. It works best if someone is coming at you with great force, perhaps with two hands, to grapple you. You use the force of his own arms to bounce your palms off his arms and into the side of his jaw. The harder they attack, the harder they are struck. You do not have to use that much power to cause a KO here.

Figure 325

Figure 326

Figure 327

Figure 328

GOVERNOR VESSEL 26 (GV 26)

The power of this point, just under the nose, can be demonstrated by having a strong person lean forward while in a strong stance. Try to push his waist to upright using his forehead, and you will find that it is almost impossible. Now, place just one finger laterally across Gv 26 and press upward. He is upright in no time at all, and you have not used that much pressure on the point. In a realistic situation, however, we attack this point with the palm heel or a one-knuckle punch. Again, a smaller person can bide his or her time until the shot is available, then thrust the palm heel up under the nose with devastating results. This strike will work even using a stiff type of attack with only triceps power, but by using the whole body in a fa-jing manner, you will kill the attacker with this point (fig. 327).

CONCEPTOR VESSEL 22 (CV 22)

This point will stop an attacker instantly. At the very least he will drop to the ground in a coughing fit, gasping for air, and at most he will die. The point can be accessed using a palm heel, the tips of the fingers, an elbow, or a one-knuckle punch. The attack should have intent behind it, using fa-jing, although it will work on a purely physical level even if you do not have fa-jing and simply strike it using brute force. For instance, if a woman is grabbed from the front, she can get an elbow into the point (fig. 328).

THE EYES

There are points in the eyes, of course, but what does it matter—the eyes are extremely sensitive to even a light scrape across the eyeball. In fact, the best type of attack to the eye is a scrape, which will produce temporary or permanent blindness and extreme pain, causing the recipient to drop. If, for instance, a woman is attacked, she uses her fingernails to strike across the eyeball on either side (fig. 329).

Figure 329   Figure 330

The above methods and points will give you more than enough to be able to defend yourself using the most dangerous methods. In the following paragraphs, I will discuss some more of the more dangerous points, some of which take a little more training than what can be learned at a day-long seminar.

THE MIND POINT

This is one of the "extra points." It is near the back of the jaw, just forward of the earlobe. It is struck at an angle of about 45 degrees to the front of the body toward the backbone. This is quite an amazing knockout point, requiring only medium power to cause KO. It is usually struck using a cross fist. You have stepped to the attacker's right, for instance, and your right fist strikes across his oncoming right attack and to the point (fig. 330). Women sometimes prefer to use a palm heel strike because the wrist of a woman, if not conditioned, could be damaged.

GALLBLADDER 3 (GB 3)

The temple is traditionally a well-known point to strike to, and Gb 3 is the temple. It can be struck all by itself to cause death or KO, or it can be used in conjunction with a qi-disruptive method of slicing the left hand across the attacker's face from his left to right. (The latter is never done in the reverse manner. Even if you attack to the other side of his head to the opposite Gb 3 point, the qi disruptive method is still from his left to right.) The point is struck straight in using a one-knuckle punch. This strike is well documented in the first volume, in the chapter on the gallbladder meridian.

CONCEPTOR VESSEL 23 (CV 23)

This point will stop any attacker when struck up and into the neck at an angle of 45 degrees. You can use a knife-edge strike or the tips of the fingers with equally devastating results.

NEUROLOGICAL SHUTDOWN POINTS

Neurological shutdown points are not really points, but rather areas of the face and neck comprising several points.

A stinging slap to the side of the jaw that includes part of the ear and neck using a palm strike will cause KO instantly. The tongue of the recipient usually turns blue and hangs out. Immediate resuscitation is required here. This area is easily accessed, and I have shown law enforcement officers that this strike works really well in controlling people. ("I only slapped him on the face, your honor"!) Should the attacker come at you with both hands, both of your palms slam the inside of his both arms outward, then your right one (or left) rebounds to strike (slap) him on the side of the face. The attacker drops immediately.

BLADDER 10 (BL 10)

This point is the old rabbit chop and works like a charm for taking someone down to his knees or flat out on the ground, depending upon how hard you hit him. It can be accessed while in a grappling type of situation with one hand around the back of the opponent's neck, using the reverse knife-edge strike to the point. The result is instant. This is one of my favorite points. You can even sucker the attacker in, until he thinks he has you, then you strike to the back of his neck. I am always amazed at how few grapplers or jujutsu people use these strikes (although, I must admit that in tournaments these strikes are disallowed because of their danger).

GOVERNOR VESSEL 20 (GV 20)

This point is not only a great revival point, it is also a wonderful KO point. A strike using perhaps the reverse knife edge upward into the skull will cause KO easily. Again, it can be used in a grappling situation.

SMALL INTESTINE 17 (SI 17)

Just under the hinge of the jaw, this point is another wonderful KO point. The knife edge or reverse knife edge is used here. It can be accessed from a choker hold or whenever you can get at the point, which is usually when you have closed with the opponent. This point was prominent in the jujutsu practitioner's arsenal in the 1940s but for the purposes of tournament fighting it was dropped and never resurrected. A sharp upward strike into the neck and chin will cause a KO, with the recipient not even knowing it happened.

TRIPLE HEATER 23 (TH 23)

I got really excited about this point when my seven-year-old son (at that time) could easily knock me out using it. This point seems to do many things, both electrical and physical, to the body. The strike is done downward over the bone at the corner of the eye, usually using a palm heel strike. (See the relevant chapter in the first volume for more information on this point.)

SMALL INTESTINE 16 (SI 16)

This is a point that is easily accessed and very dangerous. It can be got at in much the same way that St 9 is accessed, only the direction is straight in to the side of the neck. (See the relevant chapter in the first volume for more on this.)

LIVER 14 (LIV 14)

As you move down the body, this is one of the more deadly points. Located just under the pectoral crease by about 1 inch, midline down from the nipple, it is easily accessed from the front of the body, and the results are devastating. The immediate effect is collapsed lungs, resulting in KO and, eventually, death.

CONCEPTOR VESSEL 14 (CV 14)

One of the most dangerous points that stops the heart, this point, located where the solar plexus is situated, is struck straight in with a slightly upward flick.

GALLBLADDER 24 (GB 24)

Also a dangerous point that will cause KO or death, this point is located 1 inch below Liv 14, midline down from the nipple, about 2 inches below the pectoral crease. It is struck straight in.

SPLEEN 17 (SP 17)

I have experienced the pain of being struck at this point; you just have to sit down and not move, even when struck with a medium blow. Located to the outer side of the pectoral in a lateral line to the nipple (not quite under the arm), it is struck from out to in, laterally across the body, usually using an elbow.

LUNG 5 (LU 5)

This is one of the best set-up and qi drainage points I know of. Located at the elbow crease on the outside of the inner arm, it is easy to get at using the back of the palm slicing downward. It will cause considerable damage to the arm and central nervous system, as well as to the qi system of the body. This strike will cause KO.

PERICARDIUM 6 (PC 6)

You will find Pc 6, or neigwan, mentioned more than any other point in this book, because it is the best utility set-up point, causing both qi drainage and nausea. You can virtually use this point as a set-up to any other point strike. Located midline on the inside of your forearm, about one hand's width back from the wrist crease, it can be accessed via a strike or a wrist lock.

The above points are only my preferences. There are other points that are just as deadly and easy to access. It is always better to work out the ones that you prefer to use for yourself. The way to find out which ones suit you is to have someone simply attack you when you least expect it. Find out where your hands went, and you have your answer. This is where the taijiquan and bagwazhang practice of push hands comes into play. This is an excellent method of discovering exactly which points are suited to you. During advanced push hands in either martial art, we are attacked when we least expect it with all kinds of attacks and have to deal with it at a reflex level. You will find that you keep using much the same two or three methods to defend against all types of attacks. Work with these methods and the points that are located in these areas and specialize in them. In this way you can be assured that your martial art will become a truly great self-defense art; you have changed your "tools" into a system of self-defense.

I have several videos published on the taijiquan and bagwazhang ways of practicing push hands, and the taijiquan way is covered in *Power Taiji*, by Erle Montaigue and Michael Babin (published by Paladin Press).

Chapter 5

The Medical Aspects of the Martial Arts

There are certain physiological principles that *anyone* can apply to cause a KO. These principles have been known for many years in the medical field and have been well documented in books written by, among others, eminent doctors as far back as 1863. One such book, *The Medical Aspects of Boxing* (Jokl 1941), is by far the best resource ever written on the medical aspects of strikes and is still relevant today. Unfortunately, it has been out of print for many years. (This book is not to be confused with the book of the same name published in 1993, edited by Barry D. Jordan, compiling ideas and experience from many different medicos. The earlier book is light years ahead of its more contemporary publication.)

The principles outlined in Jokl's book can be and are applied by many martial artists to bring about KOs in demonstration and such, and they work very well! Is it my belief that some of these "KO specialists" got their hands on this book some years back and applied these easy medical tricks, claiming that they were a part of the martial arts all along. Unfortunately, these "medical tricks" are probably the most dangerous strikes ever, especially when the subject is a sitting duck in a demonstration!

Before I began to tell people about dim-mak, martial artists didn't know what points they were hitting or what they were called. Most only knew the general area of the strike and did not understand either why the KO happened or the dangers of such strikes, done even lightly.

In dim-mak we apply these medical principles and also the principles of qi flow in the body in conjunction with the acupuncture points. So dim-mak makes use of these medical tricks to cause KOs and other damage to the human body, but it also delves much deeper into the energy system of the body, and this is what separates the men from boys, so to speak. The person who has only learned some medical tricks can never advance beyond that; the knowledge and training are just not there. On the other hand, the person who has studied the whole art of dim-mak will continue to develop and give out his knowledge until he dies. It is very interesting to note that in all the books I have read on the medical tricks that can cause KOs, the authors simply admit that there are certain human phenomena that they cannot explain using Western medicine. And this is where the energy system strikes come into play. Dim-mak has an answer for every strike and its consequences, which, more often than not, go way beyond purely physical phenomena.

When one knows about dim-mak and has the ability to put in or take out adverse qi, then certain combinations of strikes really will cause dramatic energy changes in the body, producing effects ranging from nausea to KO to death! But it takes years of training to gain this ability, and by that time one has neither need nor the desire to ever use these attacks on anyone. The advanced practitioner wishes only to help others by advancing his or her own healing ability through the study of dim-mak.

I have had hard-style black belts come to me asking me to teach them the strikes! How can I possibly show them about dim-mak when most of them do not even know how to move, let alone punch! One must have complete control over his own body and mind before he can enter the realms of the higher levels of dim-mak. Sure, I can show people the medical tricks, and then they can go back to their students and knock them all out with a light blow here or there, but *can they do it in a fight?* The answer is no, because they have not done the training required to learn how to fight, first of all, which takes more than just a few katas and sparring matches and a couple of tournament wins.

There are certain points that will set up other major points, such as Pc 6 struck before a St 9 shot. This will cause the brain to send a lot of qi and blood to the wrist area, thinking that something really bad has happened to the whole body because the Pc 6 point indicates what is happening in the body. This leaves St 9 vulnerable for a strike, which will cause the carotid sinus to react and shut down the heart, because it thinks there is extreme high blood pressure. Co 10 will cause a KO all by itself struck hard enough, as will the mind point, but put the two together and you have a dangerous strike indeed. But you shouldn't try to remember the combinations of strikes; this would not work in a fierce fighting situation since you would not have enough time to think about what combinations to use. Through training, the strikes must become totally subconscious, where the mind just knows about where to strike and the body does the rest. The dim-mak training is such that we teach people how to defend themselves first by utilizing the reflex reactions of the body. Only then can a student go on to learn about dim-mak and how to use it. Just learning about the points means nothing, and anyone is able to cause a KO by using basic medical principles. But if you wish to delve more into dim-mak, it requires much study and training under the guidance of someone who knows about dim-mak, and not just the simple medical procedures.

KINKING THE BRAIN STEM TO CAUSE KO

Many "KO specialists" would have us believe that they are using combinations of points to cause certain KOs—points that they alone know about. For instance, a KO can be done very easily by causing the brain stem

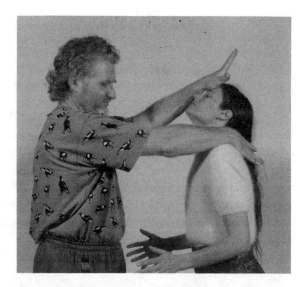

Figure 331

Figure 332

Figure 333

to kink. This type of KO is well known in boxing circles when a strike to the chin has been landed. The martial artist can pretend to be striking, for instance, Gb 14 along with Gb 20 (fig. 331). In this case, the brain stem is simply kinked, and a KO will occur very easily. It has nothing at all to do with the fact that the practitioner's hand was near or on Gb 14 or Gb 20; it is simply a medical trick. The hands could have been anywhere on the forehead and back of the neck pulling and pushing and it would have had the same effect. The strike to Gb 20 will work fine all by itself if you know about dim-mak! However, without an understanding of the energy systems of the body, you will have to rely on a medical trick, also using, for instance, Gb 14. The Gb 14 strike has nothing at all to do with the total strike electrically but simply causes the brain stem to be kinked. The same goes for Gb 20 and St 3—both points work really well all by themselves, with St 3 capable of causing great nausea and Gb 20 causing KO. If, however, you push the head backward by striking to St 3 as you strike to Gb 20, you will cause the brain stem to kink, causing KO.

Any way that you can get the brain stem to kink, such as a sudden pushing back of the head, will cause KO, and this is why, when certain irresponsible individuals strike their students or workshop attendees at the inside of the elbow, they will cause KO. The brain stem has again been kinked by the action on the arm, which causes the head to be forced backward violently (fig. 332). This is why the old rabbit chop works so well to cause KO—it causes the brain stem to be kinked (fig. 333). Same thing with a quick little strike under the chin with a knife-edge strike. Again, it causes the brain stem to kink, causing KO.

THE HEART KNOCKOUT (CONCUSSION OF THE HEART)

It is interesting to note that the following well-documented experiments (Jokl 1941) were conducted in Germany between 1931 and 1933. This material is not for the faint of heart, since it involves doing damage to rabbits and dogs with hammers!

Schlomka carried out a well planned series of experiments in which he demonstrated that blows against the lower part of the left anterior chest wall [Liv 14, St 15, St 16] may provoke a variety of pathological circulatory reactions. Schlomka used anaesthetised rabbits and dogs, which he subjected to blows with a wooden hammer against the chest wall. In contradiction to certain theories which had previously been advanced, Schlomka showed that the shock which frequently follows thoracic injury is not usually due to tears of the heart valves or to haemorrhages into the heart muscle.

The typical sequelae of a well placed blow to the left side of the chest as observed in animals (rabbits and dogs) can be described as follows: arterial blood pressure falls abruptly, e.g., from about 100 mm. Hg. to 30 mm. Hg. and less, while venous pressure rises sharply from 18 mm. Hg. to 50 mm. Hg. and more. These two reactions alone clearly indicate a profound disturbance of circulatory integration. Electrographic tracings taken during the experiment show that the normal rhythm of the heart is suspended and that series of pathological contractions of the cardiac muscle set in.

In all cases that were radiologically investigated, acute dilation of the heart was found In some cases, the size of the heart increased within a few seconds by between fifty and two hundred and fifty percent. As a rule, the phase of acute shock was followed by spontaneous recovery, which terminated the effects of the blow. In a few cases the heart, after having spontaneously recovered for a second time, slowly increased in size; circulation gradually failed, electrocardiographic tracings became grossly abnormal and all the animals in the group died!

A few animals died directly on receiving blows to the chest. Basing his opinion on his autoptic findings, Schlomka arrived at the conclusion that it is the nervous mechanism of the heart which in such cases becomes paralysed In ninety percent of the animals, no gross anatomical changes in the heart were discovered.

In dim-mak we know that strikes to the heart region will cause trauma. The strikes to St 15 and St 16, for instance, will not only have an effect directly upon the heart by their location, but will also affect the vagus nerve, which has endings in the lower stomach wall. Again, medical science is at a loss as to explain why the KO sometimes occurs with only a medium blow to either side of the chest. Dim-mak has the answer: the vagus nerve ends in the stomach, and when it is either attacked directly, as in a blow to the stomach, or indirectly by an attack to St points elsewhere on the body, KO is caused by the action on the vagus nerve.

THE SOLAR PLEXUS KNOCKOUT

The following also comes from *The Medical Aspects of Boxing* (Jokl 1941).

> In 1863, Professor Goltz, who was at that time in Konigsberg, carried out experiments on frogs which are now considered classic. In his original publication in Pfluger's Archive No. XXVI (1863), Goltz described an experiment which since then became known as "Goltz's Klopfversuch."
>
> Using frogs (medium sized rana esculenta), he cut small windows into their thorax without injuring the pericardium, thus being able to watch their hearts beating. By tapping against the frog's abdomen, he induced the heart to beat slowly and ultimately to stop in diastole. At the same time, respiration became suspended. Goltz stressed that the tapping was so slight that it did not cause any injury to intestinal organs.

In dim-mak we know that a strike to Cv 14 will cause the heart to stop because of its physical proximity to the solar plexus and also because it is an electrical point on the Cv meridian, which causes the upper and lower parts of the body to become separated electrically. So not only does this deadly strike have a physical action upon the heart, as in Goltz's experiments, but it cuts off the qi (electricity) to the heart, causing it to stop with little hope of revival, even using CPR.

The conclusion of the above experiment was that the strike to the solar plexus area (Cv 14) caused "an afferent nervous impulse travelling through the spinal cord to the medulla oblongata, from where it switched over to both vagus nerves which then carry it to the heart." Goltz also found that even if the intestines were pushed aside and the spinal column tapped directly, it had no effect. But when the intestines were placed back into position and tapped, the heart stopped! Tapping on other parts of the intestinal tract had equally positive results. So Goltz established that there are receptors situated in the intestines and stomach themselves and that strikes to these areas (as we now know) cause KO or death.

In dim-mak and acupuncture, those who also investigated striking certain points in the body back around the year 1300 A.D. came to these conclusions. But because they did not have the scientific knowledge that we have today, they simply said, for instance, that a strike to St 9 or to the solar plexus (Cv 14) caused either KO or death.

THE THUMB IN THE NECK

Another classic medical trick—one that most older jujutsu practitioners would know about—is the old thumb-in-the-neck trick. This simply involves pressing the thumb into St 9 point, causing the carotid sinus to react so that the heart rate plummets dramatically, resulting in a KO (fig. 334).

• • • • •

The above tricks can be performed by anyone who has an inclination to hurt students, but be warned: without exception, all of the books that I have ever read and all of the medical practitioners I have interviewed say that these medical tricks are *very dangerous,* with the effects ranging from loss of memory to Parkinson's disease and mental disorders.

Figure 334

Every time the brain stem is kinked it causes a little more damage, until one day the person just dies or becomes a vegetable, as so many boxers have found. *There are no safe strikes—none at all.* Even the purely dim-mak strikes that affect the energy system cause irreparable damage. They should only be used if one's life is threatened, and never, ever for demonstration.

There are many other points on the body that cause physiological effects, but their reasons for working as such have not as yet been proven scientifically. We know that they work, but do cannot explain why with Western science. All we have to go on is the dim-mak explanation of why they work.

Perhaps in years to come, someone like the above-mentioned doctors will find reason to investigate martial arts strikes further. But, sadly, many doctors have been given the opportunity to do so and have not come up with any more than what was put forth in very early works such as that written by Ernst Jokl in 1941! However, all is not lost. I have gained much information from my own training, other well respected doctors, and the two books mentioned above, and I have begun writing my own book on the subject, tentatively titled "The Medical Aspects of Martial Arts Strikes." It will cover all of the "medical tricks" in the martial arts covered in this book based on modern experiments and papers on the subject.

QI DISRUPTION: THE SCIENTIFIC ANSWERS.

I am also currently working on a book that will cover the nine qi-disruptive forms/katas of Wudang Shan that I learned in China under Liang Shih-kan (I was the first Westerner ever to learn these). These methods involve certain fa-jing movements across certain meridians of the body, "cutting them" to cause adverse electrical currents, thus affecting the power of the body without even touching the skin! I have experimented with these, and the experiments are well documented in my video series *The Qi Disruptive Katas of Wudang Shan.* The proof that they work is shown in this series against very strong people from all walks of life and people that I have only just met. The effect is devastating.

In dim-mak we know that by waving a hand across certain meridians in a certain direction, we cause the meridian to be "cut" by our own magnetic force (hand). We also know that a meridian is a conductor of electricity, and from electronics we know that when a conductor is "cut" rapidly by a magnetic field, an electromotive force (EMF) is formed across the conductor, and an ensuing current will flow if the circuit is closed. This is exactly how an electric motor or generator works. So we can cause a minute current to flow adversely along a meridian, thus (in a nutshell) causing weakness in the body. This current must be a minute one, however, because this is the level of electricity of the body. When a large EMF and current are used, the person is only electrocuted! But when a minute current is set up, the body is affected greatly and can even be put to sleep. Isn't this beginning to sound exactly like dim-mak?

We get an inkling of how these strikes work from the book *Supermemory: The Revolution* (Ostrander and Schroeder 1991).

Mapping the body's bioelectric fields, the Soviets found that "waking consciousness itself is a function of direct currents that run from negative to positive poles in the brain" . . . a central front-to-back flow in the head. By passing a low-voltage current through the front of the brain to the back, you can cancel the normal current of waking consciousness and knock a person out.

The Soviets had discovered what Dr. Robert Becker of the Syracuse VA Hospital was only to confirm decades later. Chemical anaesthesia, acupuncture anaesthesia, and hypnotic anaesthesia all work the same way. They reverse the polarities of the brain's electro-current of consciousness.

Qi disruption—the ability to control someone's qi or energy either for self-defense or healing—is one of the highest levels of the martial arts. Those who only know about the above-mentioned "medical tricks" do not know about the higher levels of the martial arts.

My main thrust for telling people about dim-mak is so that they will know about the dangers of practicing such tricks. Something as simple as a slap to the side of the neck could leave a young person crippled for life—one second of glory for the person applying the technique, and someone's life is shot! A true martial artist does not have to prove that he knows these strikes by performing them on innocent bystanders whose names he does not even know, let alone such things as their medical histories. The true martial artist cares about the health of his students and their well-being. Who gives a rat's bum if someone is able to knock out a person who is simply standing in front of him? When all is said and done, humans are the weakest of all animals. When we show off for the sake of our own egos, we only show off to other humans to show that we are in some way better than they are. Take off all your clothes and sleep out in the bush for one week in winter, without canned food, and see how you go. A mouse can do this, so how strong are those who cannot do this? But they *can* knock someone out . . . wow! We *know* that it happens and why it happens; we have seen it many times. So why keep on doing it? The only reason is for ego.

My advice, if you are unfortunate enough to have paid money for a seminar where the "teacher" knocks out people and you are not man enough to simply walk out, is to at least ask that person if he can do the same thing in a real situation and if he would demonstrate it when you attack him full-force. (And I do not mean the old stepping in slowly with a reverse punch and a loud shout; I mean as he would be attacked in the street.) And when he does not agree to this, then walk out.

I once witnessed a so-called full-contact tournament where the rules dictated that there was to be no attacks to the head by hand. Kicks were allowed. Young girls were standing toe-to-toe, slamming each other in the breasts! It would have been better had they been able to strike to the face with fists! Young lives put at risk for a sport . . . how stupid we are. These young people, 12 or 13 years of age, were trying to beat each other in the ring for the sport of it, risking permanent damage to their legs from knee kicks. I suppose the same could be said of any kind of football league, but there, at least some of the time, the combatants are not in there just to damage each other. In martial arts tournaments and boxing matches, however, two individuals are in there to inflict as much damage on each other as possible, never caring or even thinking about permanent damage to a young person's life.

This is not what the martial arts are all about. They are about learning how to defend yourself, and then, at an advanced stage, learning to heal others, and finally and most important, *knowing* yourself and whence you have come.

Chapter 6

Internal Methods

Many instructors make the mistake of using too much physical force, while others use none at all. Both approaches are incorrect for gaining internal power.

Pumping weights or using other external devices will not give you any internal power; in fact, these will hinder your internal training. Internal power is something that we can use for the rest of our lives to either help us defend ourselves against physical attack or to heal our own bodies or those of others. It is only logical that when we become old and our are on the down side of our physical lives, we can no longer depend on the super muscular strength that we had in our 20s and 30s. If you depend upon external devices to gain physical strength, then you will have no strength as you grow older.

On the other hand, people who train in a system that relies on using no physical strength at all will have no power either when they grow older. They may have relied on bending the body, for instance, in the practice of push hands to avoid an attack. I have seen people who are able to bend backward almost to the ground to avoid a push, but whose genitals are greatly exposed to a strike in doing so! The practice of bending to avoid an attack is fine when we are younger and in the confines of a friendly push hands "match," but in the street it does not happen that way. So people who practice push hands for competition will never be able to defend themselves in the street. Sport does not constitute a self-defense form. And as we become older, it is natural for some of the suppleness that we had when we were young to go. It is important to practice a martial system that has an equal amount of hard and soft, or yin and yang. Many of the taijiquan styles, for instance, have too much hardness, while others are not hard enough.

The internal is a combination of mind and body. Through training, we come to a level where the body executes exactly what the mind orders. The mind "orders" at a subconscious level, however, and the body executes at a reflex level. So there is no time between what the mind thinks and what the body does. And all this comes from what the Chinese call *sung*. The closest we can get to an English translation of this term is "to relax." But this gives the wrong impression, since relaxing conveys the idea of taking it easy, using no muscular power, and so forth. I prefer to use the term "internal tension." In this state we are not tense; the muscles are in a state of readiness but are not flexed, and there is a high degree of qi activation in the body so that we are ready for any situation.

When a subconscious reflex action occurs, the mind instantly thrusts the limbs out using the power of the waist, causing great centrifugal and centripetal power. This is the yin and yang of internal power; we must make use of outward power as well as inward power. So when you throw out a punch, for instance, this is using centrifugal power. Then just upon impact, you snap that punch back using centripetal power, causing a great whipping action on the end of the fist, which sends not only physical power but also internal adverse power into the object. You can use this type of power right into old age, provided that the training has been correct. You can, however, do an older body great damage in performing fa-jing movements incorrectly! Many instructors advocate much movement of the waist to get fa-jing. But this violent, longer movement will cause damage to the spine. Fa-jing must be so minute that the body is not seen to move much at all. In this way we do not damage the spine or the arms or the wrist.

There is an excellent way to monitor your internal power. When you first get up in the morning, really clench your fists hard. This should be easy and feel full of power. Then unclench your fists and immediately throw out a fa-jing snap punch, pulling it just before the elbow is hyperflexed. If this strike is full of great power that feels like it would kill anything that came in contact with it, then your internal power is getting there. The trick, of course, is to keep such power into older age, and this involves the more esoteric side of the internal martial arts. This is where we use phrases like "being one with d'ao" and "we enter into nothingness." I liken it to our being a large cog in a machine, and all of our younger lives this cog is not quite in harmony with the rest of the machine. Finally in older age, the mechanic gets it right and this cog makes contact with the larger cogs in the machine and the whole machine runs smoothly.

On a physical level and with reference to our martial arts training, there must come a time when we realize that physical strength will no longer aid in self-defense. Yet the body moves like a well oiled machine, loose like an elastic band, contracting and expanding at will without thinking. We are now using the power of the ground, like a great, powerful tree. This tree doesn't think, "Oh, here comes a breeze, I must defend against it"; it simply has the power and it defends against winds and storms automatically. It is the same with us—our roots have been cultivated so well through our training that we are now able to use the power of the earth to help in defending us.

QIGONG

Qigong is a way of gaining this "ground power." Look at most ancient indigenous races—they all have a way of gaining the power of the ground, and it invariably involves sinking the heels into the ground in some way. The Australian aboriginals stomp their heels into the ground, while the American Indian has the "power stance," not unlike the sanchin stance in karate.

Internal power is a state of mind that can be gained through the practice of qigong. Unfortunately, of late there has been an explosion of qigong teachers and methods. In Australia, it would seem that teachers are cropping up on every corner. People go to China and learn a set of movements, then go back to their own country and advertise that they have the answer to all of our health problems—and this after only several lessons! A qigong teacher has to have studied the art for at least 15 years before he or she can teach the internal qigong. Knowing only the physical movements of qigong means nothing; a teacher must be able to pass on the internal essence of qigong, and this can only be gained after many years of practice.

There are about 2,000 different types of qigong methods, and they can be divided into three categories.

Self-Healing

This is where the qigong exercises are used to gain good health, to cause the acupuncture meridians to be relaxed and open to allow for a normal flow of qi through them, bathing each organ in the body in life-giving qi. There are many different types of self-healing qigong, and the internal martial arts of taijiquan and bagwazhang are both considered to be moving, self-healing qigong. The basic qigong, however, is a static stance using certain breathing techniques, sometimes called "three circle standing qigong" (fig. 335).

The hands are held with the "dragon mouth point" (Co 4) activated. This is done by having a straight line of skin between the thumb and the forefinger. Simply adjust your thumb until there is only one line of skin. This will give the palm a concave, "dragon claw" type of look. The palms are held at about neck

Figure 335   Figure 336

height, around 3 inches apart. The elbows are hanging below the wrists. The tongue is placed onto the hard palate as if pronouncing the letter L, and the chin is pulled back slightly to pull the backbone up. The knees are bent so that there is a vertical line between the second toe and the knee. The base of the foot is slightly concave, which activates Kd 1 point. The gaze is straight ahead parallel to the ground. The buttocks hang naturally under and are not stuck out or forced under too much.

In this position you think about nothing at all, not even the breathing. I used to teach, as most do, to think about the breathing since this gets the mind thinking about only one thing. But nowadays I believe it is much better to think about nothing right from the beginning. Just stand there for 15 minutes, and you will feel some shaking. If you do not, then you probably have risen up slightly so no heat is created from the thighs working. It is very important that you have your weight placed over your heels or, at the very most, just forward of the heels in the middle of the foot. It should never be placed on the balls of the feet! This can cause "adverse cyclic qi," which can in turn cause some brain damage! Done correctly, however, this basic qigong stance can do no harm even if done wrong (apart from the weight distribution). You will know whether you have your weight placed on the front of your feet when you begin to jerk violently, as your body goes into spasms that come and go. This indicates that the ground qi is trying to get through Kd 1 but is blocked by the pressure on the balls of the feet, so it builds up and bursts into the body, going right up to the brain and causing this body spasm. If you get a mild shaking that is continuous, then you are doing it correctly. My videos No. MTG 10 and MTG 1 cover the basic qigong.

Martial Qigong

This type of qigong is no different from the self-healing qigong, other than it sends qi activation to different parts of the body—those parts used in the martial arts. A typical martial arts qigong is shown in (fig. 336). This type of "one-legged" qigong will increase the qi activation to both the legs and arms. It is also the qigong that you perform (on each leg) before performing your taijiquan form or karate kata training. It will enhance your training many times over.

Medical Qigong

This qigong is used by a qigong doctor to cure someone of disease. The doctor places his hands over the affected area and allows qi to be transmitted through his body into the affected area, thus helping the patient to heal himself by boosting the immune system. This is the most advanced type of qigong and should only be practiced at an advanced stage of one's martial arts training. The martial arts are practiced as a means to gaining this level of qigong. This is why I have always said that one needs to train in things like taijiquan, training in both the healing and the martial.

Qigong is also important in acupuncture, since this is where the advanced acupuncturist will be able to rise to a high level of healing by putting qi (electricity) into the points via the acupuncture needles. Training in acupuncture for years, knowing every point and what it does, is no good at all if you are not able to pass your own qi through the needles into the patient's body. (I have seen quite sick acupuncturists actually treating people! They will make their patients even sicker!)

TCM doctors should at least practice their own self-healing qigong every day to enhance their own healing ability and to strengthen their bodies so that they do not take on the diseases they are treating! All good TCM doctors in China also practice their own qigong, especially when they are treating some dire disease state. In fact, the doctor will practice his own qigong for 10 days and fast before treating a really difficult patient.

The other side of qigong's connection to acupuncture comes from the history of acupuncture, with many scholars believing that acupuncture developed from qigong. I don't know whether this is true, since I believe that it came from God! However, I will give some history of qigong and acupuncture for the sake of interest.

Qigong has been known in China since around the fourth century A.D., when the early Taoists developed their *dao yin* exercises. When advanced practitioners practice their own qigong, they feel a certain electrical flow through each meridian. This is also a theory about how the meridians were discovered; although, again, it sounds most unlikely to me, because it is my theory that it was given by God.

Qigong used to be called "guiding the qi" or "qi activation," where the practitioner focuses the mind on a certain area of the body, such as the tantien, until he attains a feeling of qi. This sensation then descends to the perineum and then up the backbone and down the front of the body back to the tantien, and this is known as ren mai and du mai communicating.

Figure 337

Figure 338

Figure 339

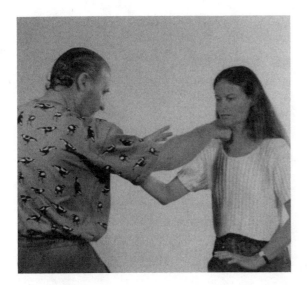

Figure 340

Figure 341

Figure 342

For many years this "feeling" of communication between the meridians was unacceptable to Western scientists. However, nowadays, they have plotted the pathways using sensitive electrical instruments, and most agree that the meridian system does exist as electrical pathways around the body.

THE MIND IN THE MARTIAL ARTS

The mind plays the most important part in one's dim-mak training. If we are to attain a high level of expertise in dim-mak, or even in self-defense, then we must rise above only the physical level of the martial arts. For instance, some of the dim-mak points, such as St 9, will work no matter how we strike them or what we strike them with. But to get the most out of all of the points, we must use the mind. When striking, for instance, to Liv 14, we can use the mind to send a shock wave of adverse qi into the heart first by the physical direction of the fist and second by the use of the mind to direct the qi into the heart. So if we strike to Liv 14 using a snap punch, where the fist begins with palm facing downward and then flicks over to palm facing almost upward upon impact (as in the use of the normal taijiquan fist), then there is an arc of qi sent upward and over to the heart (fig. 337). This will only happen if you see that arc going up and into the heart. Your mind sends adverse qi into the heart because you see that line as you attack. Once you begin to see these lines of attack, you will no longer have to even think about it because your subconscious mind will automatically send adverse qi into the targeted area, depending on which attack you use and in what direction the fist or other weapon is aimed.

You can also send adverse qi into the heart when attacking to the other side at Liv 14, by either using the other fist (in this case the left fist), or by using a different kind of punch. You use a "penetration" punch on the left side of his body, using your right fist to get this effect (fig. 338). To send adverse qi into the heart from above, you use a "reverse falling" fist to perhaps Lu 1 (fig. 339). This fist will whip downward instead of upward, not only draining much qi from the entire system by attacking Lu 1, but also sending adverse qi into the heart because of the direction of the fist.

An attack to St 9 using a "yang lateral fist" will cause KO and heart stoppage by attacking to St 9, and it will also cause heart damage by sending adverse qi into the heart (fig. 340). You can also use a "reverse falling lateral fist" to the opposite St 9 point, causing the same effect (fig. 341).

Any strike to the midline of the torso below the heart will damage the heart when you are using an "upward snap punch." This punch will send adverse qi straight up in a straight line, so when you are attacking to, for instance, any of the Cv points below the heart, it will send adverse qi straight upward into the heart (fig. 342).

You will get to know the correct angles of each punch and your fist will act accordingly. For instance, if you were to attack lower down than Liv 14, your angle of attack would automatically be less than if you attacked to Liv 14.

A knife-edge strike to St 9, flicking upward upon impact, will cause great brain damage as well as stopping the heart. The direction for this strike is still in toward the backbone, but just as the palm makes contact it flicks upward, causing adverse qi to go into the brain (fig. 343).

To cause adverse qi to go straight through the body into the points on the back, for instance, there is only one type of fist—the "vibrating" fist or palm. This is probably the most difficult of all weapons to learn. First, you must have complete relaxation (sung) in your arm and palm (fist). When you strike, the power is so great that it causes a ripple to move down the forearm into the palm, which will vibrate violently upon impact, sending adverse qi right through the body. This type of dangerous attack is used in what are called "the mother applications" from taijiquan (on one of my *Dim-Mak A to Z* series tapes). Here we use the one-knuckle punch to Cv 22, vibrating it upon impact to send adverse qi up into the brain, causing instant brain death. This is usually followed by a slap to the side of the neck, causing heart failure as well.

Depending upon where you strike on the torso, your fist will have to change rotation as it moves down the body to get the effect of penetrating the body. So if you are striking the upper body, the fist will be almost vertical with the thumb upward. As you move down the body to around Cv 14, the fist will turn downward slightly at an angle of about 45 degrees. As you get to the tantien area, the fist will be facing the ground, and as you get to the groin and lower abdomen area, it will be almost small finger facing upward. This last fist is used in several places in the old Yang-style taijiquan form.

A strike to St 5 can cause permanent brain damage as well as KO. St 5 is one of the easiest KO points, just on the side of the jaw. It works in two areas when simply stuck straight in and in three areas when adverse qi is put in. The simple KO occurs because a

Figure 343

Figure 344

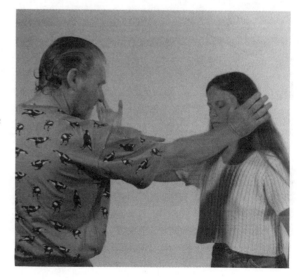

Figure 345

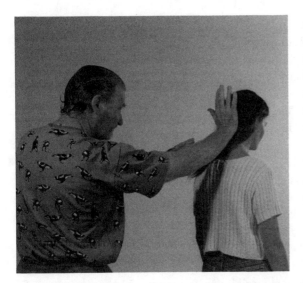

Figure 346

normal strike to this point shocks the brain, which then shuts the system down. It will also cause KO by the action on Gb 14, to which St 5 is connected, as well as the direct effect upon the vagus nerve, which has endings in the base of the stomach. The strike to St 5 causes the vagus nerve to tell the heart to either slow dramatically or stop altogether.

St 5 becomes really dangerous, however, when we use an adverse qi strike to the point. This will send adverse qi up into the back of the brain, causing permanent brain damage. This is achieved by using a "back-flicking palm." Your opponent might attack, for instance, using both hands. The stronger he is, the more powerful your strike will be because you use the ricochet effect. Both of your palms will attack to his both neigwan points, releasing yin (negative) energy into the points. The palms were yang-shaped to begin with, and just upon impact they flicked out to form yin-shaped hands, thus releasing the stored yin qi (fig. 344). This will set up the St 5 point. Now, your right palm, which is now stored with yang qi, will release that qi into St 5 point upon impact. The palm will also make a slight extension toward the back of his neck so that the adverse qi will rise up into the brain (fig. 345).

The same kind of brain damage will occur when we perform an "upward moving palm" into the base of the skull from the rear. The palm releases yang qi into the base of the brain, which rises into the brain and causes damage (fig. 346).

The above is just a tiny part of a very deadly area of dim-mak. And as I have said from the beginning of the first volume of this encyclopedia, *these techniques are extremely dangerous!* I have had people phone me or write, saying that such and such a point is their favorite KO point! How do they know this? Have they done it on someone? Perhaps on their students?! You are playing with fire when you strike to any of the points around the neck and head. It's probably just as well that these people do not know and are never likely to know about how to put in adverse qi, or their students would be dying all over the place! Someone from one of the big "KO" schools in the United States once called me a wimp because I would not knock out my students. Well, to this I simply say, "If that is being a wimp, then a wimp I will remain." And I will repeat, one of the main differences between such schools and myself, my system, and the way I teach and relate to the martial arts, is that I *am* afraid to hurt my students.

All of this involves methods that take years to gain, and it is most unlikely that anyone who is training in a "tense" martial art will ever attain the internal methods. So to those who criticize the fact that I speak openly about these most dangerous methods, my response is this: it does take years of hard training to be able to use these most deadly methods, and by that time, one has risen to a high level of being so that all he wishes to do is heal people and not hurt. However, and here is the rub, one *must* rise to this level in the martial arts in order to heal at a higher level. Long before those who have taken up the martial arts for nefarious means have reached a sufficient level to be able to use the higher levels of dim-mak, they will have dropped out, because the internal martial arts simply do not allow people with bad characters to attain the higher levels

THE 10 KEYS

There is another reason people with suspect characters will never attain the highest levels of the internal martial arts: the 10 keys are the only way to unlock the internal and the doors to the highest levels of dim-mak. The first six keys are given by the instructor over a number of years, whereas the last four are gained through hard work. The student must never know when he will be given the keys, since he will then expect something to happen, and so it will not. On the other hand, if the student is given a key and is not told about it, things will happen to his or her training long after the key was given. We have had cases where students were given a key and months later phoned to say that strange things were happening to their training. One student who was trying to have a baby with his wife for years unsuccessfully went back home after one camp and, *voila,—un bébé!*

No. 1 key is a touch here and a touch there—perhaps the teacher will find a reason to work with the particular student he thinks is ready for a particular key. He will use that student, and in demonstrating some technique perhaps, will touch the arms or torso in a certain way. No. 2 key is in words, and No. 3 key is in showing and "internal learning qi" movement. Keys 4, 5, and 6 are combinations of the above. Successfully taken, these keys will then grow, until the last four keys will just happen, turning the appropriate "locks" in the practitioner's mind and body until the internal is finally understood. The internal knowledge cannot be taken or given without the keys. `

TAIJIQUAN IS THE MOTHER

Many martial artists dabble in other such practices as yoga, reiki, and Alexander. Many are in awe of these methods when they are first introduced to them and try to convert others to this or that "new" method. Usually, as their training increases and their understanding of taiji increases, they realize that all these other practices exist within taijiquan, because taijiquan is the mother of all. Taijiquan has every other alternative healing or meditation method hidden within its framework. Sometimes it takes a few years of training for these to emerge, and that is why many do not see that taiji has everything you will ever need—because they are not advanced enough at that time to see it.

Over the years I have been exposed to most of the world's leading experts in things like yoga and reiki and Alexander technique, and I have never found anyone who was doing anything different than what is found in one's taiji practice. Yoga has some areas of taiji, and so do all of the others, but not one has it all as taijiquan does. I will cover some of the areas of taijiquan that you may not know about even if you have been practicing for 30 years. In fact, I have known people who have been training for that time and who know only one-tenth of what taiji is all about. And I am one who knows about this since I have had a life-threatening disease for many years now—one that my mother died from but which I have been able to control through my taijiquan practice.

Practicing taijiquan does not only mean practicing the form each morning or training in push hands twice a day; it is a whole integrated art comprising many different parts. Should you leave even one of these parts out, you will not gain the total benefit that taiji has to offer. This is where people go wrong. They go to their local "master" knowing nothing themselves, putting their total trust in this master. The master might *think* he knows it all and might really think that he is doing his student some good, but all the while he knows only a fraction of what taiji has to offer. They put on a little black or white "taiji suit" and learn a few movements, something they can show to their friends, and they come out after one or two years knowing taiji! My own students now know why there is the saying, "It takes three lifetimes to learn taijiquan." The information and training just keep on coming; it never stops. This is the reason for my putting out so many tapes, some that I might only ever sell 10 copies of, so that people will have some access to the whole realm of taiji training.

Obviously, not everyone is able to travel to Australia to train personally with me, and this is where I am a little sad, because I am unable to travel long distances through time zones any more to teach. Often, students will only be able to come to Australia for our annual WTBA training camp once every two years. So they have to be content with learning from video and by voice and e-mail contact in the meantime. Because of this, some students feel the need to take up some other practice, not knowing that all the while it was there in their taijiquan. They just have not come to the advanced stage as yet to be able to take it all in. It is impossible to understand the internal area of life unless you have been training in the internal arts for at least 15 years. So I scoff when I see other therapies offering "mastership" in one year! I personally know of people who, after only six months of training in other therapies, have come out with a master's certificate! Heal yourself first! Only then can you even think to begin healing others!

TO KNOW

How do you know if your teacher knows it? Do not rely upon knowledge, do not rely upon the amount of moves he knows, do not rely upon how good at self-defense he or she is, do not rely upon how many big words he can rattle off in one sentence, do not rely upon how the "master" is dressed. Only ever rely upon the attitude of the master—his calmness, his giving nature, his concern and care for his students, and, mostly, whether or not you feel good just being in close contact. This is the test of a real healer. Remember how good it was to cuddle up to your mother's breast when you were one day old? Of course not, but your subconscious sure does, and that's why we love to be close to other humans—the subconscious desire for that warm glow from your mother. This is what the master has also; when you move close, there will he a warm glow that pulls you closer subconsciously. Often there will be nothing physical to tell whether a person is a master, and this is the first sign that perhaps he is! A "master" does not look like a master but just an ordinary person at first. But the *power* is there.

What is taijiquan?
    It is a martial art.
    It is a method of self-defense.
    It is a meditation.
    It is a self-healing method.
    It is a method of healing others.
    It is a scientific method of medicine.
    It is a method of scientific diagnosis.
    It is a method of physical exercise.
    It is a method of mental exercise.
    It is a method of balancing one's yin and yang energies.
    It is a method of gaining spiritual awareness.
    It is a method of finding "The Way," or correct path.
    It is a method of achieving longevity.
    It is a method of aligning one's magnetic fields with the earth.
    It is a method of communicating with God.
    It is a method of eating the correct food.
    It is a breathing exercise.
    It is a method of thinking the right thoughts.
    It is a method of doing unto others as you would have done unto you.
    It is a method of investing in loss in order to gain.
    It is a method of helping others.
    It is a method of gaining "the power" to change things.
    It is the ultimate self-defense, in causing others to do what you want them to.
    It is a method of love of all things.

And you thought that taijiquan was only a physical exercise.

Medical

Glossary

The following medical reference is by no means complete. I have only included the anatomical terms and the disease states that are included in this encyclopedia and that most people would not be familiar with.

A

Addison's disease: This disease is caused by failure of the adrenal gland to secrete corticosteroid hormones and can be life threatening. Addison's disease (or syndrome) can be caused by a number of factors, such as tumor, autoimmune diseases, and infection.

    Indications of this disease include weakness, a change in color of skin (mainly to a darker shade), cold sensitivity, loss of appetite, weight loss, and intestinal problems, to name a few. There is a Western treatment program that cures this disease.

adnexitis: A swelling of the adnexal organs of the uterus, i.e., the fallopian tubes and ovaries.

amenorrhea: The normal flow of blood and discharge called menstruation does not happen. Normally, for instance, during pregnancy and milk flow or before puberty and after menopause, this flow does not occur. However, with amenorrhea, the flow does not appear at all or stops for unnatural reasons. The former is normally caused by malfunction with the hypothalamus gland, the ovary or uterus, or the pituitary gland. The latter often occurs in athletes who achieve an extremely low percentage of body fat as a result of intense training and in women who have eating disorders.

ametropia: We get a wrong image at the back of the eyeball because the light is not bent the correct way upon entering the eye.

angina pectoris: A pain in the chest like a cramp that travels down the left side of the body, usually caused by a lack of oxygen to the heart. It is also linked with hardening of the arteries. The patient feels like he or she is dying from suffocation.

anhidrosis: An absence of sweating when one should be sweating under normal stimulus.

aphasia: Speech is lost due to a nerve problem, usually caused by injury or disease in the left side of the brain. It is not a problem of articulation, etc. It can be reversed, and in most cases speech returns.

aphonia: Loss of voice caused by disease of the larynx or mouth. It can be caused simply by overuse of the vocal chords.

apoplexy: Nowadays, we simply us the word "stroke." Apoplexy is a stroke with paralysis.

ascites: This disease can be caused by a number of factors. Mainly, though, it is caused by cirrhosis (liver disease). It is an abnormal amount of fluid in the abdominal cavity with large amounts of protein, and swelling of the abdomen.

atelectasis: The failure of a part of the lung to expand, as seen in many premature babies. It can happen in adults from inhaling foreign bodies or from bronchial cancer or tuberculosis, an internal blockage, etc. Physiotherapy can help this situation.

atrophy: Part of the body wasting away. This can be caused by disease or accident. Muscles can atrophy simply form lack of exercise. Restricted blood flow is also a factor.

B

borborygmus: Noises from within. Bowel or stomach noises, rumbling, or gurgling noises. Usually caused by a blockage of the small intestine.

beriberi: Is a dietary deficiency disease cased by a lack of vitamin B. The disease is characterized by neuritis, often with muscle atrophy, poor coordination, and eventual paralysis. Death may occur from heart failure. The disease is prevalent in those parts of the East where polished rice is the main food. Health is restored quickly when adequate amounts of vitamin B are given. (Also called "leg qi.")

Buerger's disease: An inflammatory condition of the arteries, especially in the legs, that predominantly affects young male cigarette smokers.

C

canthus: The corner of each eye where the upper and lower eyelids meet.

cholecystitis: Inflammation of the gallbladder, usually caused by a bacterial infection that results in great pain over the Gb and fever. Acute cholecystitis is usually associated with gall stones. An X-ray is usually taken to rule out other diseases, such as appendicitis.

choroiditis: An inflammation of the choroid layer of the eye (the layer of the eyeball between retina and sclera).

chorioretinitis: The outer membrane and retina of the eye are swollen, usually due to inflammation. Blurred vision and light sensitivity are some symptoms.

chyluria: Chyle in the urine. This gives a milky appearance. Chyle consists of certain digestive juices, which make their way into the urine from the small intestine.

conjunctivitis: Inflammation of the front of the eye, called the conjunctiva. Caused by infection, bacteria, or virus and spreads quickly to the other eye and to others who have close contact. Swelling, redness, and pus will also be present. This disease causes more discomfort than pain, and it can affect vision, but this is rare. (Also called pink eye.)

costal: Relating to a rib, near a rib.

Costalgia: Pain in the ribs. This term is very rarely used nowadays. (I guess they simply say, "Pain in the ribs"?)

Cushing's disease or syndrome: Overstimulation of the adrenal glands by excessive amounts of ACTH/corticosteroid hormones secreted by a tumor of the pituitary gland. Symptoms are excessive body hair growth, weight gain, reddened face and neck, osteoporosis, (loss of minerals from the bones), high blood glucose levels, and often mental disorders. This can also be caused by the use of steroid drugs over several weeks or longer.

D

dyschezia: Constipation caused by a voluntary urge not to defecate over a long period. The bowel is distended, and defecation is difficult and painful.

dysuria: Difficult and painful urination due to a bacterial infection of the urinary tract. Frequent urge and urination. It is usually helped by a large intake of fluid. This is a symptom of urethritis, cystitis, or proctitis.

E

edema: An excessive level of fluids in the body tissues. This used to be called dropsy, and years ago people would die of this disease. It is not that prevalent nowadays and is easily treated.

empyema: Pus in a body cavity, such as in the area between the lung and the membrane surrounding it. Caused by an infection like TB or pleurisy.

endometritis: Inflammation of the endometrium (the mucus membrane lining the uterus) caused by chronic or acute infection. It may also be caused by foreign bodies, such as parasites or bacteria. Sometimes happens after childbirth or abortion where the woman is fitted with an IUD.

enuresis: Lack of control over urination, usually in the evenings in bed.

epilepsy: Can be any one of a number of disorders of brain function. Characterized by sudden attacks of convulsions, or blackouts, or seizures, or all three. There is an uncontrolled discharge of electricity from the nerve cells on the surface of the brain. The cause is generally unknown.

F

febrile: Means the high temperature of the body as a febrile reaction to infection.

furuncle: This is a localized staphylococcal skin infection, usually occurring in a follicle of the hair. Pain and red swelling that exudes dead tissue. (Also called boils.)

frontal cortex: This is the most complicated part of your brain. It is responsible for intellect, personality, and learning. Judgment and reasoning and consciousness are also produced here. This area is directly affected by environment and upbringing.

G

glaucoma: High blood pressure within the eye. The normal flow of fluid between the cornea and aqueous humor (lens) is blocked. Acute glaucoma can result in blindness within two to five days; chronic glaucoma may take years to develop. Usually controlled by eye drops.

goiter: A swelling in the neck caused by an overgrown thyroid gland.

H

hemafecia: The presence of blood in the stool.

hematuria: A presence of blood in the urine at an abnormal level, caused by kidney diseases.

hematemesis: The act of vomiting blood.

hemiplegia: One side of the body is paralyzed.

homeostasis: The constant state within the body that is is naturally maintained, comprising body temperature, heartbeat, blood pressure and production, salt balance, breathing, and glandular secretions.

hypermetropia: Farsightedness. Near vision is more blurred than far vision.

hyperosmia: High sensitivity to smells.

hypochondriac region: Both sides of the upper abdomen and beneath the ribs.

hypoglossal nerve: A pair of nerves in the head that cause tongue movement and swallowing.

hyperopia: Same as hypermetropia, farsightedness. (U.S. terminology.)

hyperosmia: A high sensitivity to smells.

I

ischaemia: The organ or part of the organ that receives inadequate blood supply caused by some restriction in the blood supply.

inguinal: Pertaining to the groin area.

K

keratitis: Inflammation of the cornea of the eye.

keratoleukoma: A firm nodule that appears mainly on the face and grows to 1 to 2 centimeters across in about six weeks.

L

lacrimation: Crying, or simply tearing. An excessive amount of tears as in crying.

lassitude: Wanting to sleep all day, no energy, etc.

leukorrhea: A white or yellowish discharge from the vagina. This can be normal during periods or during pregnancy.

lumbosacral plexus: The nerves that supply the legs and pelvic area.

lymphadenitis: Usually caused by a bacterial infection or circulating cancer cells causing inflammation of the lymph nodes.

M

micturition reflex: The urge to urinate. This is normal when the pressure of fluid rises in the urinary tract. Controlled naturally but uncontrolled as with infants.

menorrhagia: Longer and heavier than normal menstruation periods. Happens naturally at some time in a woman's reproductive life. If it continues, she should be checked out for cancer, etc. It may cause anemia if left too long without help.

myopia: Shortsightedness. Distant things are blurred.

myocarditis: Inflammation, either acute or chronic, of the heart muscle.

N

nebula: A scar or "spot" on the cornea, usually not causing light to be blocked. It is picked up only by an optometrist using specialized lighting.

Nelson's syndrome: A hormone disease that could follow the removal of the adrenal gland. Many call this disease Cushing's Disease.

nephritis: Kidney disease of any kind that has swelling or organ malfunction as its symptoms.

nephroptosis: Dropping of the kidney into the pelvis. This can occur in very thin women, for example.

neuralgia: Pain caused by diseases that affect the nervous system. (It is usual to place the affected portion of the body placed before "neuralgia," as in "facial neuralgia.")

neurasthenia: Psychological and physical conditions causing fatigue, irritability, headache, anxiety, dizziness, and intolerance to noises. Can be caused by a head injury or neurosis.

neurosis: Any long-term behavioral or mental disorder in which the patient is aware of it. (In other words, the patient maintains a connection with reality.)

neurodermatitis: A skin disorder usually found in anxious or nervous patients. The skin—especially around the forehead, forearms, nape of the neck, and legs—is hard and thickened as a result of scratching or rubbing.

O

ophthalmoplegia: Paralysis of the muscles of the eye. Can be either internal or external.

orchitis: Inflammation of the testis, either one or both. Can cause sterility if caused by mumps.

otorrhea: Any kind of discharge from the ear. Usually seen in chronic middle ear infections.

P

palpitation: A very fast beating of the heart in some people who are under stress and in heart patients.

pannus: The outer layers of the cornea become filled with blood vessels, usually as a result of inflammation of the cornea.

pancreatitis: A swelling of the pancreas, which can be caused by damage to the gallbladder or too much alcohol. The acute variety is often deadly. The chronic variety is also usually caused through alcohol abuse and is associated with diabetes.

parotid glands: A pair of the largest saliva glands, situated on the inside of the cheek below the outer ear.

parotitis: Swelling or infection of one or both saliva (parotid) glands. Mumps.

peptic ulcer: A breakdown of the lining of the digestive tract. Usually occurs when pepsin and acid are at unusually high levels.

pericarditis: The pericardium, or the membrane that surrounds the heart, is inflamed. Caused by injury, cancer, heart disease, etc. There are breathing difficulties and pain in the first stages. The second stages are more serious, with fluid gathering around the pericardium and a swelling on the outside of the body around the heart.

pleurisy: Inflammation of the linings of the lungs (*pleura*, an oily membrane that surrounds the lungs). Symptoms include pain in the lungs and shortage of breath. Can be caused by pneumonia, cancer, or tuberculosis.

polupus: Same as polyp. A growth, usually benign, proturuding from the mucus membrane. Commonly found in the nose.

pronator teres: The muscle in the forearm that turns the hand down or back (as in the yin- or yang-shaped hand).

prostatitis: Infection of the prostate gland, causing swelling with the urgent need to urinate. A burning sensation accompanies urination.

pruritus: Itching, or rather that which makes someone need to scratch, sometimes causing infection.

psychosis: A mental disorder that has a physical or emotional source. The patient may have illusions (mistaken beliefs) and/or delusions (false beliefs).

pterygium: A triangular overgrowth of the cornea, on the inner side, by thickened and degenerative conjunctiva. People from dry, hot, dusty climates are more prone to this disease. It very rarely interferes with vision.

ptosis: Eyelids that droop, either one or two of them, caused by a weakness of the muscle that raises them or malfunction of the nerve that triggers this muscle.

pyelonephritis: A bacterial infection of the kidney. Characterized by fever, chills, and a need to urinate frequently, this disease moves quickly. Can lead to kidney failure.

R

rhinitis: Nasal discharge caused by inflammation of the mucus membrane in the nose. A runny nose.

rhinorrhea: Mucus freely flowing from the nose. Or the release of spinal fluid after a head injury.

S

sclera: The hard stuff behind the eyeball (membrane) that keeps the eyeball in its shape. The white of the eye.

scrofula: An old name for tuberculosis of the lymph glands in the neck.

stye: An infection of a gland of the eyelid that forms pus.

T

tachycardia: When the heart contracts at a rate greater than 100 beats per minute at a regular rate.

temporalis: The muscle that closes the jaw; one of four muscles used for chewing.

thrombocytopenia: Too few platelets in the blood, causing bleeding into the skin, bruising easily and bleeding after injury.

tidal fever: A fever that comes and goes (like the tide).

tinnitus: Ringing in the ear, which could be a sign of acoustic injury.

trigeminal neuralgia: Stabbing pain in the face along the trigeminal facial nerve. Caused by pressure on the nerve.

trismus: A long-term spasm of the jaw muscles keeping the jaw tightly shut. As in tetanus. Also called lockjaw (informal).

U

urethraliga: Pain of the urethra.

urticaria: A skin condition where the skin erupts into wheals (or welts) of differing shapes and sizes with clear margins.

uveitis: Inflammation of any part of the uveal part of the eye. Could be caused by diabetes, trauma, infection, and could turn into glaucoma.

MEDICAL GLOSSARY

Glossary

Accumulation point: Where the qi accumulates so that it can be sent to different parts of the body.

Acupressure: A way of using the acupuncture points for healing without using needles; only the fingers are used to press the points.

Acupuncture points: Along each meridian or channel, there are points that offer less electrical resistance. These are the points that an acupuncturist will pierce with a metal needle in order to put into the body, qi or electricity from his or her own body. The points in this book are numbered with a system well accepted in the West. (Usually Chinese texts are numbered differently than are Western texts.)

Chen: A family in China whose style of taijiquan is becoming more popular in modern times. Many believe that it was the Chens who invented taijiquan, while others believe that they simply changed their form of Chinese boxing to be more in keeping with the taijiquan principles. Nowadays, Chen style is regarded as one of the four major systems of taijiquan.

Cheng point: An extremity point. (Many extremity points are used as emergency points.)

Chang Yiu-chun: One of only three disciples of Yang Shou-hou and teacher of Erle Montaigue.

Chee Sau: Sticking hands. This is a training exercise in taijiquan that teaches students about hand techniques and reflex actions. Both partners join hands at both wrists and, using circling motions, try to attack each other from this short distance with punches and palm attacks. The very instant an attack is felt, the attackee reattacks, thus defending himself using an offensive method.

Chi: Ultimate, the pinnacle, as in t'ai chi ch'uan. (Do not confuse this with *ch'i,* or qi.)

Ch'i-na: The art of locking the joints. Jujutsu is a form of this. Taijiquan has its own version of it based solely upon the postures of the forms.

Chong mai: One of the eight extra meridians.

Chu King-hung: One of only three disciples of Yang Sau-chung and teacher of Erle Montaigue in the Yang Cheng-fu system.

Ch'uan: Fist, or boxing, as in t'ai chi ch'uan.

Cun: (Pronounced "tsoone.") A measurement of about 1 inch, used in acupuncture and dim-mak to locate points. The distance between the second and last knuckles on the middle finger when the finger is bent tightly.

Dai mai: The girdle meridian, which runs around the waist. An extra meridian.

Dim-mak points: The same points that are used in acupuncture, but they are used on a martial level, to kill or to heal.

Dim-hseuh: Another name for dim-mak.

Du mai: Governing (vessel) meridian. One of the eight extra meridians. Unlike the other six extra meridians, however, this one, along with the *ren mai*, or conceptor (vessel) meridian, has its own meridian and points.

Emergency points: Those points that are used in diagnostic procedures to determine whether a patient is in dire straits, or those that can be used in emergency situations, such as death.

External martial arts: Those such as karate, tae kwondo, and the kung-fu systems, such as Choy Lae-fut, Jow gar, and Hung gar, that had their beginnings at the Shao-lin temple in China.

Extra meridians: There are 12 main meridians in the body and eight "extra" ones. Whole medical practice has evolved in China using purely the eight extra meridians. These meridians also hold the key to some of the most deadly point strike combinations.

Extra point: These are acupuncture points that have either been discovered after the main meridian points were discovered or are not situated upon any particular meridian.

Extremity points: Those acupuncture points that are "at the extremities" of the body, such as Ht 9 at the tip of the little finger.

Fa-jing: Explosive energy, fa-jing is the "motor" of dim-mak. Without it, you just cannot use dim-mak. It is a way of attack using the whole body rather than just the portion of the body that is issuing the attack. It is very much like a sneeze. Your whole body sneezes, however, not just your nose.

Fen: About one-tenth of an inch, also used to measure acupuncture points.

Fu: Hollow organs, the yang organs.

He point: A sea point, or "gathering together."

Hun: The spiritual soul that lives in the liver.

Ho Ho-choy: Disciple of the great bagwazhang master Chiang Jung-chiao, and one of several teachers of the author in bagwazhang.

Ho ho ha ha kee kee ku ku: The call of the Australian kookooburra.

Internal martial arts: Those martial arts systems, such as taijiquan, bagwazhang, and h'sin-i ch'uan, that rely more upon an internal strength, making use of the flow of qi rather than relying upon brute strength.

Jeh: The will, which lives in the kidneys.

Jing point: Used for the river point.

Jing qi: The extra kidney qi that is stored in the kidneys and is used for resuscitation.

Ke, or ko: The controlling cycle of the five elements.

Large san-sau: A training exercise in taijiquan wherein both partners perform attacks and defenses in a set dance-like routine of attack and defense. Every posture from the taijiquan form is employed in this set. At an advanced stage, more free-style attacks and defenses are used.

Luo: A connecting point or meridian.

Mai: Meridian or channel.

Martial taijiquan: This is the second level of a taijiquan student's martial training. It is necessary to understand martial taijiquan in order to use it for healing others. This is where we learn how to use taijiquan for self-defense. It goes much deeper than simply knowing what each posture is used for.

Medical taijiquan: The highest level of one's internal martial arts training. This is where the practitioner is able to use taijiquan postures to actually heal someone of disease. It is not just the patient doing the postures himself, but the "doctor" using the martial arts application of each posture to heal disease.

Meridian: A channel along which "qi" (energy, electricity) flows. There are 12 main meridians and eight "extra" ones in the body. In this book, we deal with the 12 main meridians and only glance at the eight extras where necessary.

Ming: Translated as brightness or sunlight. *Yang ming*, for instance, is the sunlight yang division of stomach and colon.

MO: Abbreviation for meridian or channel.

Mu: To mobilize. Mu points are the alarm points on the meridian. Should one of these be very tender, it could indicate disorder in that meridian or organ.

Pauchi form: Cannon fist form. this is the solo version of the large san-sau. There are two sides, "A" and "B." At a solo level, the student performs the A and B sides without stopping. This is one of the best ways of learning about martial arts movement.

Po: The animal spirit, or the soul of the animal, which lives in the lung.

Push feet: The taijiquan practice of a set of movements of attack and defense practiced by two people using the feet. Both partners stand on one leg, joining the other leg at the Achilles tendon. Circling begins as one person tries to kick at the other's leg with his heel. The attackee defends by turning his body and thus pulling that attacking foot in an arc, thus forming a circle when the whole operation is repeated. At an advanced stage, hand attacks are also employed, all on one leg.

Push hands: The taijiquan practice of a set of movements of attack and defense practiced by two people using the hands. This is not a competition, but rather a training method that teaches the use of taijiquan as a self-defense art. It begins with simple pushing and defensive movements and becomes quite advanced in attack and defense. Beginners start with big, low, open stances. As they learn, the stances become more like those that would be used in a real street fighting situation. Punches, finger jabs, leg attacks are all part of this training method.

Qi: An internal energy that flows through the acupuncture meridians, bringing a life-giving force to every organ in the body. Qi is used for every movement and action of the body; without it we die.

Qigong: Literally, internal work; a means of gaining good health through certain stances used in conjunction with breathing methods. An integral part of one's taijiquan or any internal martial arts training. There are 2,000 different types of qigong, broken down into three categories: self-healing, martial arts, and medical.

Ren mai: Conceptor (vessel) meridian. One of the eight extra meridians. Unlike the other six extra meridians, this one, along with du mai, has its own meridian and points.

Self-healing taijiquan: This is where we all begin our taijiquan training. Each posture of the taijiquan form causes one of the main meridians in the body to be activated, thus beginning the self-healing process necessary for healing the internal organs.

Shao-lin: Literally, "Little Forest"—a place in China where the monks of the Shao-lin monastery would study the martial arts as part of their training. It is believed that all of the hard-style martial arts, including karate, came from this temple.

Shen: The spirit that lives in the heart.

Shiatsu: The Japanese version of acupressure.

Shou: Literally, "hand" or "arm." Can be used as follows: *Shou shao yin* means "hand lesser yin," or the heart meridian.

Shu: This is a collective term for the five welling, stream, or antique points.

Shu Point: A transporting or "stream point."

Small San-Sau: The taijiquan way of learning about the main applications of the postures of the taijiquan kata or form up to the posture known as "single whip." One person is the attacker, throwing different types of punches in a set routine, while the attackee defends against these attacks using the postures from the form. At an advanced stage, the attacks and defenses will become free-style.

Stasis: A condition in acupuncture wherein the blood is stagnant.

Sun family: Sun Luc-tang learned several taijiquan systems and also bagwazhang and h'sin-i ch'uan. He then formed his own style of taijiquan, the "Sun system." He was better known for his bagwazhang, however.

T'ai: Meaning greater or supreme (as in t'ai chi ch'uan, or supreme ultimate boxing.) T'ai yang is the greater yang division of bladder and small intestine.

Tuite: The Japanese name for dim-mak.

Tui-na: The Chinese art of massage, which includes manipulating the acupuncture points and twisting the meridians to cause a healing.

Wudang Shan: A range of mountains in China's Hupei province that holds great religious significance to the "internal" styles of martial arts. One of the peaks of this range, also called Wudang Shan, is said to be where Chang San-feng founded the martial system of dim-mak, which later became known as h'ao ch'uan and, nowadays, taijiquan.

Wu family: Wu Quan-yu learned the Yang family system from Yang Lu-ch'an and passed it on to his son Wu Chien-chuan, who changed the system to become the Wu family system.

Wei qi: Protective energy.

Xie cleft point: An accumulation point.

Yang: In this book, we use the classical Chinese meaning for yang and yin, rather than the newer Japanese concepts of this term. So for our purposes, yang means expanding, light, male, open, warm, active.

Yang family: Yang Lu-ch'an founded the most famous system of taijiquan in the 1700s. His sons Yang Ban-hou and Yang Kin-hou also learned his system. Kin-hou's sons, Yang Cheng-fu and Yang Shou-hou, also learned their father's and grandfather's system. Cheng-fu changed it to what has become the most popular system of modern taijiquan. Shou-hou, on the other hand, refused to change the system. The author, Erle Montaigue, has trained extensively in both of these systems.

Yang Sau-chung: Sau-chung was the head of the Yang family until his death in May 1985. He was the eldest son of Yang Cheng-fu and was one of Erle's teachers.

Yang qiao mai: One of the eight extra meridians.

Yang wei mai: One of the eight extra meridians.

Yin: Dark, passive, female, closed, contracting, cool. It must be remembered that "yin and yang" can only ever be relative to each other. So Papua, New Guinea, would be considered yang to Sydney, Australia, which would be yin in this instance. However, Sydney is yang compared to Melbourne, which would be yin in this instance, and so on.

Yin qiao mai: One of the eight extra meridians.

Yin wei mai: One of the eight extra meridians.

Ying qi: Nourishing qi.

Yong point: Spring or stream point.

Yuan: Ancestral; origin or source.

Yuan point: A source point that draws upon yuan qi.

Zhang: Solid yin organ.

Bibliography

Chen, Jing. 1982. *Anatomical Atlas of Chinese Acupuncture Points*. Jinan, China: Shandong Science and Technology Press.

Ding, Li. 1991. *Acupuncture Meridian Theory and Acupncture Points*. Bejing, China: Foreign Language Press.

Jokl, Ernst. 1941. *The Medical Aspects of Boxing*. Pretoria, South Africa: L. van Schaik P/L.

Martin, Elizabeth, ed. 1994. *Concise Medical Dictionary, 4th edition*. Oxford, England: Oxford University Press.

Matsumoto, Kiiko, and Stephen Birch. 1986. *Extraordinary Vessels*. Brookline, MA: Paradigm Publications.

Ostrander, Sheila, and Lyn Schroeder. 1991. *Supermemory: The Revolution*. New York, NY: Carrol & Graf Publishers.

Rogers, Cameron and Carol. 1989. *Point location and Point Dynamics Manual*. Sydney, Australia: Acupuncture Colleges of Australia.

About

The Authors

Wally Simpson became interested in alternate health care in 1973. He earned a degree in reflexology and Swedish massage in 1977; went on to study Oriental massage, including shiatsu and Chinese massage, with various teachers in Australia, New Zealand, and Indonesia; and in 1980 set up a practice on the Gold Coast, Australia.

Meanwhile, he studied Traditional Chinese Medicine at the Australian Colleges of Acupuncture, Brisbane, graduating with a diploma of acupuncture in 1986 and a Bachelor of Acupuncture in 1987. In 1994 he received his diploma in Chinese herbal medicine.

Wally has studied and practiced yoga and meditation since the early 1970s and taijiquan for the past eight years—five of these in the Erle Montaigue system and the last two under the personal tutelage of Erle Montaigue.

Wally has always been a keen surfer and still enters into surfing competitions (at his age!). In fact sometimes on his way down the beautiful Queensland and Northern New South Wales coastline, he looks out there, pulls his car over, and has a quick surf before class. Wally used to be a "bricky," or a person who lays bricks for house building. This in itself says a lot about the man; he has experienced life—an important prerequisite for any internal healing/martial art!

Wally Simpson presently lives with his wife and child on the Gold Coast, Australia, and runs his private practice, where he has developed his own style of massage, incorporating aspects of Chinese massage, Japanese shiatsu, deep tissue massage, and manipulative techniques.

Erle Montaigue began his martial arts training when he was 11 years of age, training in karate and judo for a short while at the local police Boys' Clubs. His forte in these early years, however, was wrestling, which later led him to professional wrestling for a time. He was also an avid bodybuilder, later realizing the error of his ways.

In 1966, Erle was expelled from school for little more than being a rebel and painting the school yellow, among other "small" things. In 1967 he took up a telephone maintenance course, where he met his first teacher of taijiquan, Mr. Wong Eog.

By the late sixties, Erle was married with two children. He was performing in stage plays and with his band, and he already had a No. 1 hit record, "Can't Wait for September," to his name. He was "expelled" from the telephone job for dyeing his hair green and singing on the job, so he took up music as a profession and became a rock and roll star, having several hit records and albums to his name by the early seventies.

In 1974, while performing as a nightclub entertainer, Erle left Australia for England, where he met his second taijiquan instructor, Mr. Chu King-hung, who took Erle on as one of his first students (if not the first). Chu King-hung is one of only three disciples of the late Yang Sau-chung (1909–1985), the eldest son of Yang Cheng-fu. Erle continued his acting career while in London, performing in several plays, musicals, and films before returning to Australia at the end of 1977.

In 1981 he traveled to Hong Kong, where his form was looked at by Yang Sau-chung, and where he studied with Ho Ho-choy, a direct disciple of bagwazhang Master Chiang Jung-jiao.

In 1982, after having taken up several occupations, including professional chauffeur and cab driver, he began teaching taijiquan in Sydney and became the chief of therapeutic movement at the NSW College of Natural Therapies. He opened his own school in Sydney in 1983.

The next year, Erle found his main internal martial arts master, Chang Yiu-chun, from whom he learned the secrets of dim-mak and h'ao ch'uan (taijiquan).

In 1985, Erle and eight of his students traveled to China to become the first Westerners ever allowed to view the All China National Wushu tournament, held in Yinchuan, Ningxia. There, he was tested by three of the world's leading internal martial arts experts and was granted the degree of "Master." He was the first Westerner to receive this honor.

Erle Montaigue has his own column in *Fighting Arts International*, the prestigious British martial arts magazine, and *Australasian Fighting Arts Magazine*, one of the longest-running quality martial arts magazines. His photo has appeared on the front cover of both of these publications, as well as that of *Karate/Kung-Fu Illustrated*, published in the United States. In addition, Erle has produced several books and a video with Paladin Press. Erle's magazine articles and books have helped change the way people view the internal fighting arts, and his 120 self-produced video titles have helped students learn from quality tapes when a teacher was not available. He currently serves as the editor of *Combat & Healing* magazine and heads the World Taiji Chinese Boxing Association, which has schools in more than 30 countries.

In 1995, Erle was invited to study with Liang Shih-kan, the leader and "keeper" of the now almost extinct forerunner to taijiquan, the Wutan Shan System of Boxing, thus becoming the only Westerner and one of only a handful of people to be taught the nine qi-disruptive methods.

Today, Erle and his second wife, Sandra, live with their three children, Ben, Eli, and Kataleenas, on their farm in Northern NSW, Australia, on the caldera of one of the world's largest extinct volcanoes.

Readers wishing to contact either author directly may do so by writing to them at the following address:

MTG Video & Books
P.O. Box 792
Murwillumbah NSW 2484
AUSTRALIA

E-mail: taiji@ozemail.com.au
Web site: www.ozemail.com.au/~taiji

GV 12 (GOVERNOR VESSEL POINT NO. 12)

Chinese name:

Shenzhu (body's pillar).

Location:

Below the spinous process of the third thoracic vertebra, in the supraspinal and interspinal ligaments.

Connections:

An internal branch to Bl 12.

Direction of strike:

Straight in.

Damage:

This point is a good point to cause lung damage. Coughing fits and even asthma may be caused with this strike if left untreated. It will also have an effect upon the qi of the whole body, causing qi imbalance, which will lead to severe general illness over a period.

Set-up point:

Lu 5 or Lu 1 or 2.

Antidote:

The point to treat is the same one that was struck. This depends upon the physical damage to the area. Often, the damage must be treated first, and when this is on the mend, then the acupuncture treatment will commence.

Healing:

Innervation is by the medial branch of the posterior ramus of the third thoracic nerve. Irrigation is by the posterior branch of the third intercostal artery and the vertebral venous plexus.

Use for cough, asthma, bronchitis, pneumonia pulmonary tuberculosis, chest pain, back pain and stiffness, mental disease, hysteria, and furuncles.

Traditional indications include wheezing cough associated with consumptive conditions, heat in the chest, aphasia from apoplexia, seizures, infantile convulsions, stiffness and pain in the lumbar region.

Traditional functions: *Shen* here means body and *zhu* here means pillar. This point is below the third thoracic vertebra and connects upward with the head and neck and downwards with the back and lumbar vertebrae like a pillar of the body. Cools heat, regulates the Qi in the channels of the back, and opens the chest.

Massage techniques are the same as for Gv 3.

Use with Gv 14, Bl 12, Bl 13, Bl 43, Lu 7, Lu 8, St 40, Cv 17, Liv 14, Liv 3, Bl 17 for pertussis, bronchitis, etc. For asthma, add Cv 22, dingchuan (extra) to the above formula. Use with Th 23, Gb 20, Gb 1, Gb 14, Bl 1, St 2, Pc 7, Co 4, Co 20, Co 5, Gb 42, Gb 43, Gb 44, Gb 4, Bl 10, Gv 14, Bl 18, Bl 20, St 40, taiyang (extra), Gb 8, for conjunctivitis (be careful not to cross-infect the eyes if there is only one infected).

Applications:

Any of the previous strikes to the back points such as the points on the bladder meridian.